The True Nature of God

THE IMPORTANCE AND BENEFITS OF UNDERSTANDING GOD'S CHARACTER

by
Andrew Wommack

Unless otherwise indicated, all Scripture quotations
are taken from the *King James Version* of the Bible.

The True Nature of God
The Importance and Benefits of Understanding God's Character
ISBN 1-57778-036-1
ISBN 978-1-57778-036-6
Copyright © 1997 by Andrew Wommack
P. O. Box 3333
Colorado Springs, Colorado 80934

Contents

Introduction

Did you know that if a person really knew God and understood God as the wonderful Father He is, there would be no trouble believing Him and His Word?

There has been a great emphasis in the body of Christ in recent years on teaching faith and confessing His Word to bring faith. I believe in speaking what God's Word says, and believers need to have faith in God, but I also believe many of us have missed an important key.

Having faith in anyone means developing your relationship with them to the point where you know them so well, you just completely trust them.

A minister friend of mine once said that as he carries his little girl around, she never has to say, "I confess with my mouth and believe in my heart that my dad will not drop me. And I confess with my mouth and believe in my heart that my dad's going to feed me." For that daughter, there is no striving to believe her father is going to be good to her. She just rests and relaxes in her loving relationship with him. She knows he is going to take care of her, because she knows him and his character.

In the same way, Christians will find it is easy to have faith in God to provide their needs by simply getting to know Him better. And since everything we receive from God comes through faith in Him (including our salvation), knowing Him intimately becomes very important! Really, everything we receive from God comes out of knowing Him.

One of the reasons the Christian life has been so hard for a lot of people — and I'm including people who have heard teaching about faith and confession — is because they haven't really developed a personal relationship with God. They don't know Him intimately. When you really know a person is trustworthy, it's not hard to believe them. I personally believe that faith is a direct result of knowing God better.

It's not hard for a person who really knows God to believe Him and His Word. And when you believe God's Word, it's not hard to receive from God. But if a person doesn't know God very well, Satan can discredit God and say all kinds of false things about Him because that person doesn't know any better.

Before I get into more of this subject, I have to admit to you that I tend to minister by shock technique. One of the hardest things to get people to do is to pay attention, to really *hear* what you have to say. So to get their attention, I say things that paint me into such a corner that they're interested to find out how I'm going to get out of it. They start listening intently, and ultimately they get the point I am trying to make.

The Word of God is simple. A minister I know says it's so simple you've got to have somebody help you to misunderstand it. There's nothing hard about the Word of God. The biggest problem is that people don't really hear it. People are thinking about what they had for breakfast, where they're going to eat lunch, or about this or that. So before I explain what I believe is the nature of God, I'm sharing with you first that some of my points may seem somewhat dramatic.

For example, once I was teaching that God is not the One Who puts problems on believers. There was a man at the meeting with his 12-year-old daughter, who was a paraplegic in diapers, paralyzed and confined to a wheelchair. She was in such bad condition that she couldn't even relate to what was going on around her.

Because I had said God was not the One Who put that affliction on his daughter, this man got upset. The people who brought him to the meeting said to him, "You at least owe Rev. Wommack the courtesy to talk to him after the service and let him explain himself."

Afterwards, the gentleman came up to me and said, "God did this to my daughter. She was born this way. This is God's will for her and He's getting glory out of this."

I answered him, "No, God didn't do this. It is not God's will that a girl be in a wheelchair and not be able to function normally. That is not the way God made people." I started sharing scriptures with him, and he started sharing scriptures right back. I thought he was misusing his scriptures, and he thought I was misusing mine. It was getting to be a theological standoff, with nobody getting anywhere.

What finally broke the standoff was when I looked at him and said, "What's the matter? Don't you love your daughter? What kind of father are you? Don't you care if your daughter ever gets out of a wheelchair or not? Don't you care if she's ever normal and can run and play?"

Well, if he was mad at me before, he *really* got mad at me after I said that! I think he was at the point of punching me in the nose. He shot back, "I love my daughter! I would do anything for her. I don't have much money, but I would sell anything, I would borrow, I would do whatever I had to do to come up with the money if it was within my power to produce healing in my daughter."

At that point I said, "And you think God loves her less? You think God, with all His power, is going to just sit back and withhold His healing from her because He wants to afflict her to teach somebody something?"

You see, that man could argue with my doctrine, but when I presented God as a father to him, he saw God's will to heal his daughter. When I applied the concept of God as a loving, caring father, the man didn't have anything left to argue about. He saw that God is our good Heavenly Father Who doesn't want His daughter paralyzed. It just wiped out all of his anger.

Understanding that God is a good God and that He loves us takes away the effectiveness of Satan's weapons against our faith. You may have been believing and praying for healing, and you know that the Word says, **...by whose stripes ye were healed** (1 Peter 2:24). You probably know all about faith teaching, how to confess the Word, and all the related principles. Yet you've got this nagging doubt that you can't overcome. It is a fear inside that makes you wonder, "Is God really going to heal me?"

Did you know fear would be totally cast out of your thinking if you understood the perfect love of God for you? First John 4:18 says, **Perfect love casteth out fear.** If a person becomes fearful, wondering if God's will for their life is actually going to come to pass, then they don't really understand and know God and His immense love.

If God loves you enough to send His only Son to die for you, then doesn't He love you enough to bring about His will in your life if you are being obedient to Him? You may know some things *about* God, but if you really *knew* God's love for you, you wouldn't doubt Him so easily or question His willingness to help you. He couldn't be discredited so easily if you really understood how much He cared for you. Can you see that?

Our human relationships are imperfect, so they aren't a perfect parallel to your relationship with God. But I have good enough relationships with some people that if you came to me and told me they were criticizing me and saying negative things about me, I wouldn't believe it. That's because I know them. We've got such a good relationship established that, if they were upset with me, they would come talk to me about it. I know they would do that, so you just couldn't lie to me about them.

If somebody came and told me that my wife Jamie had been unfaithful to me while I was traveling in ministry, you would just be "barking up the wrong tree." I know my wife so well. *I know my wife.* Somebody may think, "Well brother, you just can't be sure; you never know." Well, if that's your reaction, it just shows the lack of relationship you have with your mate. It is possible to come into relationship with someone to the point that you know what they would be like and what they would do in any set of circumstances.

Our relationship with God is no different. He wants us to be assured that we can trust Him to act in our best interest no matter what the situation. And that is what this book is all about: getting to know God so well that no one can talk you out of His goodness towards you.

Chapter 1

Is God Schizophrenic?

One reason God can be so easily discredited is because people don't really know Him by His Word. The only way you can truly know anything about God is through the Bible. Everybody on the earth has an opinion about what God is like and what He will do. But the only thing He gave us to know Him — and the only source that is truly reliable — is His written Word.

Most Christians don't read God's Word on a regular basis. They just get a little here and a little there — maybe some from a preacher on TV and then a little on Sunday morning from their church. But that is not going to be enough to make a real difference in their life, and specifically in their understanding of God and His nature.

Some people do read and study God's Word on a fairly regular basis. But even then, there are a lot of passages in the Bible that appear to give a "schizophrenic" revelation of God. I'm just being honest with you! Of course, God is not schizophrenic, but that is the way it appears to some people from a casual reading of the Scriptures.

In one scripture, God commands you to be stoned to death for picking up sticks on the Sabbath day (see Numbers 15:32-35), and then in another He forgives and does not condemn a woman caught in the very act of adultery (see John 8:3-11). Examples like that have given people a rather strange impression of who God is.

The Old Testament Is Incomplete

The Word of God does not contradict itself. There is a perfect harmony to it all. Much of what is in this book purposes to harmonize the Old and the New Testaments to reach a better, more complete understanding of the nature of God.

In the Old Testament, we see a picture of God that is incomplete. It is not incorrect; it is just incomplete. People who create their understanding of the nature of God only from the Old Testament usually do not end up with a fully accurate picture. The Old Testament is only a partial picture. It is not a perfect representation of God. Unless you understand the New Testament and are able to harmonize it with the Old Testament, you are going to end up with a misunderstanding of the love of God and the whole nature of God.

One night I had a dream that I was Joshua in the Old Testament. I was going into the Promised Land, and God had commanded me to kill everybody in all of the cities, just like He commanded Joshua. That was hard for me to do! No women, children, or anything that could breathe were to be left alive. But I couldn't justify it. I was nearly to the point of saying, "God, I just can't do it."

To make the situation worse, I discovered that one of my very best friends was in one of these cities, and I was supposed to kill him, his wife, and his kids. I woke up from the dream thinking, "God, I can't do it. God, there's no way I can do it." I thought about the dream all morning, meditating on it and praying about it. I was thinking, "God, how could these things have happened?"

My answer was found by looking at the Old Testament through the revelation of the New Testament. God began to show me that if Jesus had lived in His human form in the Old Testament, He would not have done things the way Joshua did. That is not to say that Joshua was wrong. He was obedient to God and

God was operating in the manner He had to operate during that time period.

Still, all that God did through Joshua was not a true and complete representation of His nature. Nor was it Who God has revealed Himself to be to believers in the New Testament. And yet some people have the impression that God is a God of wrath Who will wipe out anyone who gets in His way.

Wanting to be a great man or woman of God, many Christians go back and begin to emulate some of the Old Testament examples. Any time you start talking about somebody being a prophet or say they have the anointing of a prophet, that person usually begins getting hard and cruel. They think they are acting like Elijah, an old bony-fingered prophet who would stick his finger right in your face and let you have it. People think of Elijah as someone who would rebuke you, lambaste you, starve you out with famine, or burn you out with fire to teach you something.

Now there are some examples of true prophets who were not hard and cruel, but when people think of the typical prophet, they usually have an impression of someone like Elijah. Young believers who think they are prophets believe they are God's lightning rod in the earth — they are going to attract all of the judgment and wrath of God and smite people if they get out of line. But that's not a total understanding of the ministry of the prophet — and certainly not of God's nature.

Under the Old Testament, you see some things being done in that manner, but that is not the whole nature of God. It is vital to know Who it is we are really dealing with. If you don't know God's nature or really understand Him, then you'll never effectively walk in the blessings and the power of God. I don't care what scriptures you learn or whose teaching you sit under. As I have said before and will say many times throughout this book, you have to come to a place where you really know God and have an intimate relationship with Him.

Religious ideas, arising from a misunderstanding of Scripture, block people from entering into a close relationship with God. Many of us are really afraid to come before God because we have been taught or have gotten the impression He is going to "hit" us with something. So many believers feel they have to bow and scrape and duck every time they come before God. That's not the relationship God desires or that His Word teaches.

Old Testament Judgment

In 1 Kings 21:1-24, Ahab and Jezebel are probably two of the most wicked people in history, and certainly the most corrupt king and queen of Israel. They conspired together to kill an innocent man named Naboth in order to acquire his vineyard. They had Naboth stoned to death and his body thrown into a field, where the dogs came and licked up his blood. While Ahab was walking through his new vineyard, he saw Elijah the prophet and said, **Hast thou found me, O mine enemy?**

Elijah replied, **I have found thee: because thou hast sold thyself to work evil in the sight of the Lord.**

Then Elijah began to rebuke Ahab and said, **Thus saith the Lord, In the place where dogs licked the blood of Naboth shall dogs lick thy blood, even thine. The dogs shall eat Jezebel by the wall of Jezreel.**

It took awhile for those prophecies to come to pass. Ahab was killed in a battle and when he was brought home, the people went to wash out his chariot. As they were washing it, the dogs came and licked up Ahab's blood. (See 1 Kings 22:38.)

As for Jezebel, when a man named Jehu became king, she was thrown out of a tower and landed on the ground by the wall. Jehu rode his chariot back and forth across her, mutilating her body. Then he went into the palace, sat down, and began to eat. Right in the middle of his meal he said something like, "Well, she's a king's daughter, and even though she was a wicked woman, she ought to be buried."

So Jehu sent some people out to bury her, but all that was left was her head, hands, and feet. The rest of her had been eaten by dogs! (See 2 Kings 9:30-37.) Elijah's awesome prophecies came to pass exactly the way he had said — so you wouldn't want to mess with Elijah, right?

In 2 Kings, chapter 1, we move on to the story of Ahaziah, the son of Ahab. Ahab and Jezebel had sinned against God to such a degree that Elijah, who was a prophet of God, had declared the terrible way their lives would end. Ahaziah had seen those prophecies fulfilled, but he didn't like Elijah any more than his parents had.

Ahaziah was following right in the footsteps of his parents. He wasn't seeking the one true God; he was seeking after pagan gods. When he gets sick, instead of seeking God and inquiring of Him for his healing, Ahaziah sent messengers to Baalzebub, the god of Ekron.

According to 2 Kings 1:3-8, when Ahaziah's messengers were on their way to inquire of this pagan god, Elijah met them and said:

> **Is it not because there is not a God in Israel, that ye go to inquire of Baalzebub the god of Ekron? Now therefore thus saith the Lord, Thou shalt not come down from that bed on which thou art gone up, but shalt surely die. And Elijah departed.**
>
> **And when the messengers turned back unto him, he said unto them, Why are ye now turned back?**
>
> **And they said unto him, There came a man up to meet us, and said unto us, Go, turn again unto the king that sent you, and say unto him, Thus saith the Lord, Is it not because there is not a God in Israel, that thou sendest to enquire of Baalzebub the god of Ekron? therefore thou shalt not come down from that bed on which thou art gone up, but shalt surely die.**

> **And he said unto them, What manner of man was he which came up to meet you, and told you these words?**
>
> **And they answered him, He was an hairy man, and girt with a girdle of leather about his loins.**
>
> **And he said, It is Elijah the Tishbite.**

The king knew it was Elijah and he was seized with fear, so he sent his armies out to capture him. Verses 9 and 10 say,

> **Then the king sent unto him a captain of fifty with his fifty. And he went up to him: and, behold, he sat on the top of an hill. And he spake unto him, Thou man of God, the king hath said, Come down.**
>
> **And Elijah answered and said to the captain of fifty, If I be a man of God, then let fire come down from heaven, and consume thee and thy fifty. And there came down fire from heaven, and consumed him and his fifty.**

That's pretty strong, isn't it? You just didn't "mess" with Elijah. Ahaziah sent out an army — fifty men and a captain over them — to take Elijah, but Elijah called fire down out of heaven and destroyed the king's men. Continuing in verses 11 and 12:

> **Again also he sent unto him another captain of fifty with his fifty. And he answered and said unto him, O man of God, thus hath the king said, Come down quickly.**
>
> **And Elijah answered and said unto them, If I be a man of God, let fire come down from heaven, and consume thee and thy fifty. And the fire of God came down from heaven, and consumed him and his fifty.**

That's 102 men! Somebody might think, "Well, Satan must have done that." But it says in verse 12 that it was the fire of *God* that came down from heaven. Elijah had access to the power of God to such a degree that he could consume people. He could kill people with the power and the anointing of God. This is similar to Revelation 11:5, where it says the two witnesses will have the power of fire coming out of their mouths, destroying anybody who stands against God.

God, in defense of Elijah, released fire from heaven and killed 102 men. Finally, the third captain and his fifty men came, but this captain was a God-fearing man. A paraphrase of what he said is, "Have mercy on me. All I'm doing is what the king told me to do." So God told Elijah to go down with him to Ahaziah.

God protected Elijah, and he wasn't touched by any of the king's men. He didn't have to call fire down out of heaven to strike anybody else. Did you know that's not the only way Elijah could have handled the problem? But this is an Old Testament example of the power, the anointing, and the wrath of God in defense of one of His prophets.

New Testament Grace

Now let's compare this story of Elijah with Luke 9:51-53:

And it came to pass, when the time was come that he should be received up, he stedfastly set his face to go to Jerusalem,

And sent messengers before his face: and they went, and entered into a village of the Samaritans, to make ready for him.

And they did not receive him, because his face was as though he would go to Jerusalem.

It had been commanded by God that Jerusalem be the center of worship for the Jews. (See 2 Chronicles 6:6.) That's where He put His temple and where the ark of the covenant was located. God had commanded His people to worship Him *only* in Jerusalem.

There was a time when the children of Israel rebelled against God and He allowed the northern ten tribes to be taken into captivity by the Assyrians. The two southern tribes, Benjamin and

Judah, remained undisturbed on the land because they had maintained worship in Jerusalem.

After the northern tribes were taken captive, the king of Assyria sent colonists from Assyria to inhabit the land of the northern ten tribes so the fields wouldn't go to waste. These colonists intermarried with the remnant of the ten tribes who had remained behind. The remnant of the northern tribes forsook their identity as Jews and intermarried with the Assyrian pagans, in direct disobedience to God's commandment not to marry people who did not worship Him.

Because the Assyrians didn't know the ways of God, the beasts of the field began to multiply. The Bible says in 2 Kings, chapter 17, that God sent lions among them. The people were being killed and devoured. The Promised Land that was a blessing of abundance to the Jews now began to produce beasts which were devouring the Assyrians.

Word of this situation was sent to the King of Assyria. He released some of the Israelite priests to return to the Promised Land and teach the Assyrians the ways of the God of Israel. If they pleased God, they would not be consumed by the wild animals.

The Assyrian colonists began to learn the outward practices to please God, but they didn't change their hearts. They were still pagan worshipers and they incorporated their pagan practices into the Israelite rituals. They did the necessary things to appease God and get rid of the wild animals, but it was not pure worship of God.

As a result, the northern tribes became a mixed race of people called Samaritans, which led to racial problems in Israel. The devout Jews who were living in Jerusalem hated the Samaritans who had corrupted worship. This is verified in John, chapter 4, where Jesus talks to the Samaritan woman at Jacob's well. There was a tremendous hatred involving religious and racial prejudice between the Jews and the Samaritans. The Jews would have no dealings with the Samaritans at all.

By Luke, chapter 9, Jesus had already ministered to the Samaritans. He had seen the entire city of Samaria respond to Him. They had accepted Him as Messiah. But now, when He came through their town, they would not receive Him because it looked like He was going to Jerusalem to worship with "those hypocrites down there." The Samaritans rejected Jesus because of His association with the Jews, a rejection based upon religious and racial prejudice.

To reject Jesus under those conditions was pretty serious, and His disciples, James and John, had a knee-jerk, Old Testament reaction:

> **And when his disciples James and John saw this, they said, Lord, wilt thou that we command fire to come down from heaven, and consume them, even as Elias did?**
>
> **Luke 9:54**

Certainly James and John were as justified in wanting to kill the Samaritans for their rejection of Jesus, as Elijah was justified in calling fire down out of heaven to kill the soldiers who had rejected the God of Israel in 2 Kings 1:10. This was a serious rejection of the Lord Jesus, and they were simply imitating Elijah, a great man of God.

The two disciples were taking a scriptural example, acting on the Word of God, and doing what Elijah did. Yet how did Jesus respond to His loyal, zealous disciples?

> **But he turned, and rebuked them, and said, Ye know not what manner of spirit ye are of.**
>
> **For the Son of man is not come to destroy men's lives, but to save them.**
>
> **Luke 9:55,56**

Jesus rebuked James and John for trying to do what was done under the Old Testament. He rebuked them for trying to be like Elijah, one of the most powerful men of God who ever lived under the Old Testament. Does that mean Elijah was sinning in

2 Kings, chapter 1? No, because at that time God was dealing with man in a different way, the only way He could at the time.

Harmonizing Old and New Testaments

When people don't look at the whole Word of God, examining the Old Testament in light of the New Testament, they generally get an Old Testament picture of God as a God of wrath, judgment, and punishment. That is *a* truth about God, and those who don't accept the love and forgiveness of the Lord Jesus Christ will one day experience a terrible day of God's judgment. But wrath and judgment are not the essential *nature* of God.

God's nature is not judgment. You can't find that in the Word of God. He does judge, and He is just and holy, but Scripture reveals to us in 1 John 4:8 that **God is love.** *Love is God's real nature*. He doesn't just *have* love or *operate* in love. God *is* love. Love is the true character of God.

Elijah's actions in obedience to God were not the complete representation of the nature of God, and the Old Testament cannot give us a total revelation of God by itself. We need the New Testament to understand the fullness of God.

In the beginning was the Word, and the Word was with God, and the Word was God.

And the Word was made flesh, and dwelt among us (and we beheld his glory, the glory as of the only begotten of the Father,) full of grace and truth.

John 1:1,14

Jesus saith unto him, Have I been so long time with you, and yet hast thou not known me, Philip? he that hath seen me hath seen the Father; and how sayest thou then, Show us the Father?

John 14:9

Jesus is the walking, living Word, and when we see Him we see the Father. So the problem many Christians are facing in knowing God is that they are seeing God through the Old Testament instead of through Jesus. They misunderstand and are confused about who God really is and the relationship He wants with them because they see Him according to the Old Testament.

In the Old Testament, God had to deal with mankind and sin in a different manner. We will study the scriptures that tell us that in the following chapters. But when Jesus came, He brought the true revelation of the Father to mankind, and He operated very differently.

I personally believe if Jesus had come to earth in His human form in Old Testament times, He would have rebuked Elijah, Joshua never would have killed every man, woman, and child in those cities in the land of Canaan, and Moses would have been rebuked for a lot of the things he did.

You may be thinking, "Brother, how can you say such things?" I believe it's clear in the Word of God that it never was God's desire to have to deal with mankind so firmly. That never was His real nature and character. But because we haven't known this, we have a mixed impression of God. We haven't seen Him in His fullness.

Most of us don't really recognize or understand the depth of the love, mercy, and compassion God has towards us. And this mistaken impression of God keeps us at arm's length from Him. That's why it is so important to harmonize all of the Word of God. Only then can you get a firm understanding of His true nature.

God, who at sundry times and in divers manners spake in time past unto the fathers by the prophets,

Hath in these last days spoken unto us by his Son, whom he hath appointed heir of all things, by whom also he made the worlds;

Who being the brightness of his glory, and the express image of his person, and upholding all things by the word of his power, when he had by

himself purged our sins, sat down on the right hand of the Majesty on high;

Being made so much better than the angels, as he hath by inheritance obtained a more excellent name than they.

Hebrews 1:1-4

In verse 3, it says Jesus is the brightness of God's glory and the express image of His person. In other words, Jesus is an exact representation of God, His true nature revealed.

In the following chapters, we are going to see that the love, mercy, and forgiveness God offers to us in the New Testament through Jesus Christ were always available to mankind, even in the Old Testament. But man's response to God's goodness in the Old Testament forced Him to deal with mankind more harshly than He desired. And, as we harmonize the Old and New Testaments, we are going to see clearly — God is not schizophrenic!

Chapter 2

God's Grace in the Old Testament

Y ou are probably asking, "Well, if Jesus is the true nature of God, just exactly *what* was God doing in the Old Testament?" The Word of God tells us clearly what God was doing.

For until the law sin was in the world: but sin is not imputed when there is no law.

Romans 5:13

When we use the term "Law," we can be referring to all of the Old Testament, but the Law used in context of this scripture is more specific. When we say Law here, we are referring to the Mosaic Law, which includes the Ten Commandments, judgments, punishments, and all of the ordinances and ceremonial observances.

Romans 5:13 shows us that before the Law, or before the Law of Moses was introduced, sin was in the world, but sin is not imputed where there is no Law. The word "impute" means to take what you have done and apply it to your account, or to hold transgressions against you. In other words, sin was not being held against people until God gave the Law to Moses.

Grace Extended After the Fall

Most people's concept of God is that the moment sin entered the Garden of Eden, the wrath of God began to be released upon mankind. People believe that God was holy and man was unholy, so therefore God separated man from Himself and drove Adam and Eve from His presence because His holiness could not stand to look upon sinful flesh. But there was a period of time from Adam until Moses when God dealt with people out of love, mercy, and forgiveness instead of wrath and judgment.

Now, of course, I believe God is holy, and I know that man is sinful, but God's love is so great that He did not just expel man from His presence. As a whole God dealt in mercy towards man, and He did not impute their sins (hold those sins against them) until the days of Moses, when the Law was given.

Sin entered the world when Adam and Eve fell to the temptation of the serpent in the Garden of Eden. Let's take a good look at how God dealt with them.

> **And the Lord God said, Behold, the man is become as one of us, to know good and evil: and now, lest he put forth his hand, and take also of the tree of life, and eat, and live for ever:**
>
> **Therefore the Lord God sent him forth from the garden of Eden, to till the ground from whence he was taken.**
>
> **Genesis 3:22,23**

When you see the word "therefore," you're always supposed to look and see what it's *there for*. So "therefore" means this verse is tying in with what was said previously.

"Therefore" links the expulsion of Adam and Eve from the Garden with what was just said. What would happen if God didn't send them out? The reason God sent Adam and Eve out of the Garden was because He didn't want them to eat of the Tree of Life, which would mean all of mankind would live forever in their sinfulness. It was not because God couldn't tolerate mankind.

Adam and Eve transgressed against God, but God did not expel them from His presence. The presence of God *went with Adam and Eve* and their descendants outside the Garden of Eden. I'm going to show you that even after Adam and Eve sinned and left the Garden, God was still walking and talking with them in the cool of the evening. He was still fellowshipping with them. Contrary to what most people have thought, a holy God was still fellowshipping and present with sinful mankind.

The reason God sent Adam and Eve out of the Garden was because He loved them so much, He didn't want them to partake of the Tree of Life and live forever in a body that was corrupted by sin. Sin gave Satan the opportunity to put sickness, disease, and all kinds of curses on us. Can you imagine what it would be like to have cancer destroying your body, and yet because you've eaten of the Tree of Life, you couldn't die? Can you imagine what it would be like to live for all eternity with diseases destroying your body, yet you couldn't die from them? It was God's mercy that sent mankind out of the Garden and away from the Tree of Life.

For a person who knows God and accepts His provision, there is a glorious, glorified body coming that won't be subject to the things this earthly body is subject to now in this life. There's coming a body better than Adam and Eve had after they sinned. God sent them out of the Garden because He didn't want them to live forever in a corrupted body, subject to all of the things we are subject to because of sin.

In Genesis, chapter 4, we see that God was still fellowshipping with mankind after the Fall, outside the Garden. We know that because God was talking to Cain and Abel. How did Cain and Abel know to bring a sacrifice? How did they know to bring a blood sacrifice and give the firstfruits of their labor to God?

Adam and Eve didn't have blood sacrifices explained to them in the Garden, because they had no transgressions to atone for yet. The Bible doesn't say this outright, but it's evident to me that God was still talking with Adam and Eve and with Cain and Abel. He was talking and communicating with them, because they understood about sacrifices and how to approach Him.

After Cain and Abel offered their sacrifices, Genesis 4:5 says, **But unto Cain and to his offering he (God) had not respect.**

It says God did not respect Cain's offering. How did they know God did not respect Cain's offering?

If you and your brother came and offered a sacrifice today, how would you know which one God respected and which one God didn't? As born-again Christians, we have a witness of God in our spirit. But Cain and Abel weren't born-again Christians, so they didn't have God inside them. It's evident God was talking to them. They were aware God was walking, talking, and fellowshipping with them, because in verse 6 it says, **The Lord said unto Cain.**

Here we have God speaking in an audible voice to Cain just the same as God did with Adam and Eve in the Garden of Eden.

> **And the Lord said unto Cain, Why art thou wroth? and why is thy countenance fallen?**
>
> **If thou doest well, shalt thou not be accepted? and if thou doest not well, sin lieth at the door. And unto thee shall be his desire, and thou shalt rule over him.**
>
> **Genesis 4:6,7**

God is talking face-to-face with Cain and Abel. As I stated earlier, most people thought God had to separate man from His presence because man was unholy and God was so holy there could be no fellowship. That's the concept most people have developed, but it's not proven or taught by Scripture.

When Cain saw God respected Abel's sacrifice more than his, he was overcome with jealousy and killed Abel in anger. The Bible shows us that God spoke to Cain about it.

> **And the Lord said unto Cain, Where is Abel thy brother? And he said, I know not: Am I my brother's keeper?**
>
> **Genesis 4:9**

Now stop and think about this. Here's the very first murderer on the face of the earth and, while he still had the blood of Abel on his hands, an audible voice from God out of heaven said, "Where is Abel, your brother?"

What would you do if you just murdered somebody, still had the murder weapon in your hand, and God spoke to you in an audible voice? You would probably die of a heart attack! You might do a lot of things, but you wouldn't just turn around and say, "I don't know where he is, God. Am I my brother's keeper?"

Do you know why Cain did that? Because he was used to talking to God. He talked to God every day. It wasn't unusual. There had to be a familiarity with the audible voice of God. God was still walking and talking with man, even after sin entered the world and mankind was expelled from the Garden of Eden. He was not imputing sin or holding their trespasses against them. God was not treating them the way the Old Testament Law reveals sin should be treated. He was operating in love, mercy, and forgiveness.

Still, God showed His disapproval of Cain's killing Abel and let Abel know what the consequences would be.

> **And now art thou cursed from the earth, which hath opened her mouth to receive thy brother's blood from thy hand;**
>
> **When thou tillest the ground, it shall not henceforth yield unto thee her strength; a fugitive and a vagabond shalt thou be in the earth.**
>
> **Genesis 4:11,12**

Cain became fearful and in Genesis 4:14 he said, "God, I'm going to be a vagabond, wandering throughout the earth, and everybody who finds me is going to try to kill me." Do you know what God did? Instead of bringing judgment on the very first murderer on the face of the earth, God put a mark upon Cain and protected him.

> **Whosoever slayeth Cain, vengeance shall be taken on him sevenfold. And the Lord set a mark upon Cain, lest any finding him should kill him.**
>
> **Genesis 4:15**

Now isn't that contrary to popular religious ideas? God did not approve of the sin, but He protected the first murderer on the face of the earth! In contrast, under the Old Testament Law, if a man went out and picked up sticks on the Sabbath day, God commanded the man to be stoned to death. (See Numbers 15:35.) God protected Cain, who murdered a man, but He commanded Moses to stone to death someone who just picked up sticks on the Sabbath day!

Doesn't that look inconsistent? It looks like the man who picked up sticks on the Sabbath day got the wrong end of the deal! The reason it looks that way is because until the Law came, God was not holding mankind's sins against them. He was overlooking (not imputing) sin as it pertained to man's fellowship with Him.

The Effects of Sin

In Genesis, chapter 3, we read about sin entering the world. Of course, you know the story. God created Adam and Eve, He was fellowshipping with them and walking with them in the cool of the evening. Satan beguiled Eve into sinning and Adam knowingly sinned against God. When they saw they were naked, they hid themselves from God. Right after they ate of the fruit, Genesis 3:7,8 says,

> **And the eyes of them both were opened, and they knew that they were naked; and they sewed fig leaves together, and made themselves aprons.**
> **And they heard the voice of the Lord God walking in the garden in the cool of the day: and Adam and his wife hid themselves from the presence of the Lord God amongst the trees of the garden.**

Why do you think they hid themselves? Why would you have hidden yourself? I'm sure there are a lot of things we could say, but it ultimately was their fear that there was going to be some retaliation from God. They were ashamed of what they had done, so they hid themselves.

Notice the Scripture doesn't say that when Adam and Eve ate of the tree of the knowledge of good and evil, they received total revelation of all of the depths of sin. My personal belief is that it took mankind thousands of years to explore and discover the depths of sin. They didn't just instantly come into the full knowledge of all kinds of sin.

I believe Adam and Eve, by our standards, even after they sinned, were still so pure that it would have blown most of us away. It didn't say they understood anything about perversion. I don't believe Adam and Eve knew that there was such a thing as divorce. If anybody ever had a justification for divorce it was Adam, but he lived with Eve for 930 years after the Fall. I believe one of the reasons for this is because originally Adam didn't know there was any other option. Adam didn't know there was divorce.

Nevertheless, even though God was not imputing sin to mankind and it took awhile for people to figure it out, sin had devastating effects on mankind from the very beginning. Sin was not only a transgression against God, but it also created an open door for Satan to come into a person's life. Sin has both vertical *and* horizontal consequences.

Sin's vertical effect is a transgression against God. Until the Law came, however, God was not imputing man's sins to him, and sin did not have an effect on man's fellowship with God.

Sin's horizontal effect is that it allowed Satan access to your life in some form. Even though God wasn't bringing judgment fully upon sin before the Law, sin was still destroying the human race.

Know ye not, that to whom ye yield yourselves servants to obey, his servants ye are to whom ye obey; whether of sin unto death, or of obedience unto righteousness?

Romans 6:16

The Word of God shows us that every time a person commits sin, they give Satan a direct inroad into their life. Even though God wasn't bringing full judgment upon sin, sin allowed Satan to come in and destroy the human race — physically, emotionally, mentally, and spiritually.

1. Diminished Life Span. In the days of Adam, people lived to be up to 969 years old. Two thousand years later, in the days of Noah, God said in Genesis 6:3, **My spirit shall not always strive with man, for that he also is flesh: yet his days shall be an hundred and twenty years.** God was not setting a maximum life span on people, because Noah himself lived to be over 600 years old. Abraham, who was born after that time, lived to be 175. Moses lived to be 120. Under the inspiration of the Holy Ghost, Moses is the one who wrote in Psalm 90:10 that a man's years shall be 70 or 80 years. Obviously, sin was diminishing a person's life span.

Why did people in the beginning live to be up to 969 years old? I believe it took awhile for Satan to get them convinced that they were supposed to die. They didn't know how to die. They had never seen anybody do it before. They didn't know you're over the hill at 30 or 40! They didn't know that at 65 you're supposed to retire. They didn't know that there was a flu season that came around every year. They didn't know about the Swine Flu, the Hong Kong Flu, cancer, and heart attacks. If they had a pain, I'm sure they didn't even know what it was. They just kept right on going. They didn't know how to submit to sickness and disease. It took a long time for Satan to get all this knowledge across to them. The only thing the Bible says they knew when they ate of the tree of the knowledge of good and evil was that they were naked.

2. Nakedness. Did Adam and Eve lose their clothes when they ate of the tree? Of course not! Adam and Eve weren't one bit more naked after they ate of the tree than they were before they ate of it. Some people would say, "Wait a minute. They were clothed in a robe of righteousness." Well, I don't think that's a good comparison because, literally speaking, they weren't wearing a robe of righteousness or anything else.

It says in Genesis 2:25, **And they were both naked, the man and his wife, and were not ashamed.** They didn't have a stitch of clothes on before they sinned or after they sinned. They weren't any more naked after they sinned than they were before they sinned. What changed was their *perception* of it. All of a sudden they *knew* they were naked. They had never thought about it before. They were never conscious of their nakedness before.

Mankind was created to be so God-conscious that they honestly didn't even notice themselves. There was no self-consciousness. They were totally God-conscious, not self-conscious. That's the way God created us to be — to be so conscious of Him that we didn't even know if we were clothed or not. None of us have ever become that God-conscious, have we? But that's the way God created Adam and Eve.

> **And the Lord God called unto Adam, and said unto him, Where art thou?**
>
> **And he said, I heard thy voice in the garden, and I was afraid, because I was naked; and I hid myself.**
>
> **And he said, Who told thee that thou wast naked?**
>
> **Genesis 3:9-11**

Do you think when Adam said, "I was afraid because I was naked," God replied, "Are you really naked? You're kidding." Do you think that's the first time God noticed they were naked? Of course not! God knew they were naked. God created them naked. But He knew they didn't realize they were naked before they sinned.

Now you may be wondering, "What does being naked have to do with anything?" To us, that may not look like a really good reason for Adam and Eve to hide themselves. But according to the Scripture, that's the only thing they recognized which made them run and hide from God. What was the big deal?

I think the reason this is so important is because God wasn't naked. God was clothed. Did you know there is no reference to

God or an angelic being in all of the Word of God where God or an angel is naked? They're always clothed! God wears garments. Did you know, in Revelation 19:8, we're going to wear clothes throughout all eternity? You're going to have an actual robe of righteousness that's made out of something like white linen that will shine. No one in heaven goes around naked.

3. Fear of Rejection. Adam and Eve were now fully self-conscious, which made them fully vulnerable to evil, and I believe the most immediate result was a fear of rejection. They were accustomed to seeing God and angelic beings clothed, then suddenly when they ate of the tree of the knowledge of good and evil, they recognized they were not clothed. When you recognize you're different from other people, a carnal, natural reaction is always fear — fear you're going to be rejected.

Rejection over being different is the root of all racial prejudice. In my opinion, it is really an ignorant thing for a believer to have racial prejudice. If Christians would just use their heads, they would realize that in heaven they are going to be with everybody! I think it is stupid to think that a person is substandard because of the color of their skin.

Nevertheless, at times, all of us can feel that fear of being different. I've been invited to speak in black churches where I was the only white person there. Even though I knew they loved me, I just couldn't help but think they might treat me a little bit differently. People are usually just a little bit hesitant when they are aware they are different from everyone else.

That's the reason there is so much peer pressure in society. Why does everybody want to be like everybody else? They want to be accepted! God created us for acceptance, to be loved just as we are. He didn't make us for rejection. Nobody likes rejection. People hate rejection because it hurts.

God didn't design you with the emotional capacity for rejection. You aren't supposed to get to where you just live with it. You can and should get to the place where rejection won't overcome you because you learn how to give it over to God. But there are people who have joined gangs, committed murder, and done every kind of terrible thing simply to be accepted.

When you recognize you're different, there's a fear that if you're not like everyone else they may not accept you. So we all tend to gravitate toward what's considered average or normal to please people around us.

The moment Adam and Eve sinned, they recognized they weren't like God anymore and they feared rejection. They feared wrath and retaliation coming upon them. It's my own personal opinion that it broke the heart of God to think that the creation He made would be so fearful of Him that they wanted to run and hide from Him. But that's what a knowledge of sin does.

4. Forever in Debt. Knowledge of sin will make a person feel guilty, and when a person feels guilty, they avoid the one they are indebted to through their sin. To illustrate this, let me share an example of a time when I owed a woman some money. She was my landlord, the vice president of a bank, and I owed her a month's rent.

I had told this woman that I knew I owed her the money. I said, "I'm sorry. I promise you I'll make it good even if I have to sell my wife's blood." (My wife's blood was worth $125 a pint.) I had promised her I would make it good. This lady was really nice to me and she said, "Don't worry about it. I trust you. I know you'll make it good." She was as nice as she could be, but I knew that I had defaulted on what I had owed her and I felt bad about it.

One day I was walking down the street and I saw her coming. When I saw her, I ducked into an auto store, even though I didn't have a dime in my pocket. I couldn't have even used the pay phone, but I went in and started looking like I was going to buy something so I could avoid meeting this woman on the street. Now she would have extended nothing but love, mercy, and forgiveness to me, but because I knew I was in debt to her, I didn't want to talk to her. That was a negative situation to me and I didn't want to face it.

If you would be honest, you would agree it is the same with all of us. We don't like to be around people who constantly remind us of negative things in our lives, and the mere mention of God — the One to Whom we owe everything — will have us running for the hills if we have sinned.

Knowledge of sin — the knowledge of good and evil — will make you want to run *from* God instead of *to* Him. Adam and Eve should have run to God when they sinned instead of running from Him. But that's the same thing we all tend to do. We run from God and try to get away from Him when we sin or feel unworthy.

5. Deception. Another important effect of sin is that it also blinds or deceives people. The Bible says in Hebrews 3:13 that our hearts become hardened through the deceitfulness of sin. Men's hearts were being hardened to the things of God in the Old Testament. They were getting so far away from God that they were justifying all kinds of sinful actions.

In 2 Corinthians 10, the Bible says it is not wise for people to compare themselves to other people. That scripture instructs us that it is not smart to measure yourself against those around you. Perhaps you have heard people say, "Well, if those old hypocrites down there at church make it to heaven, I'll make it!" Well, this scripture says that's not a very good measuring stick. What if the hypocrites down there at church don't make it to heaven?

Throughout history, people have attempted to justify their sin by finding someone who is "worse" than they are to compare themselves with. People will look at the sorriest example in the whole church and say, "If they go to church and are making it to heaven, I'll make it." That's a terrible standard of comparison. People aren't going to be measured by the hypocrites at church. People are going to be compared to Jesus! (See Romans 3:23.) Unless they measure up, they need a Savior. But it is human nature for people to compare themselves to others to excuse their sin.

Homosexuality used to be totally unacceptable by anybody's standard, even in the world. But now even some politicians —

people in public positions who are supposed to be respected — openly advocate that lifestyle. This recent phenomenon has changed a lot of people's opinion towards it because they compare themselves to others saying, "Well, if so-and-so is doing it, or so-and-so doesn't have a problem with it, it must not be so bad." The only problem is, that politician never was your standard of comparison. It is a grave mistake to openly advocate something God condemns just because someone advocates it — no matter how rich and powerful they are or what position they hold.

Why do we deceive ourselves into thinking it doesn't matter whether or not we sin? Let's look again at Cain. When Cain killed a man, God protected him instead of bringing wrath upon him. This was not because God approved of what Cain had done, but because of His goodness. Romans 2:4 says, **The goodness of God leadeth thee to repentance.** God wanted to show His love and mercy to the human race even though they deserved judgment. He wanted to show love and mercy in order to draw mankind back to Himself.

But man began to misinterpret what God was doing when He protected Cain instead of bringing judgment upon him. The second murderer mentioned in the Bible is Lamech, Cain's great-great-great grandson. When Lamech killed a man, he appealed to God and said, **If Cain shall be avenged sevenfold, truly Lamech seventy and sevenfold** (Genesis 4:24). In other words, "If God protected Cain like He did, certainly God is going to protect me even more." God didn't say that; Lamech said that! Do you see what was happening? Lamech was saying, "If Cain got by with murder, then I'm going to get by with murder. I'm more justified than Cain was."

People began to start interpreting God's patience and goodness as if He condoned and excused sin. People began to say, "Well, sin must not be so bad." This was never the message God intended to convey! But when sin deceives a person, they will think and do incredibly stupid things.

Why God Delayed in Giving the Law

By the time of Genesis 6:6, sin had become so bad on the face of the earth that the Bible says,

And it repented the Lord that he had made man on the earth, and it grieved him at his heart.

God is long-suffering, and for Him to grieve that He even made mankind, people must have trespassed against Him greatly. In Matthew 24:37 Jesus is quoted as saying,

But as the days of Noe were, so shall also the coming of the Son of man be.

In other words, Jesus said mankind will be sinning the same way they were sinning in the days of Noah when He returns. We have not yet seen sin in manifestation again to the degree it was in the days of Noah.

In less than 2,000 years (from the time of Adam to the time of Noah) the world became so corrupt that it has never gotten that corrupt again. I guarantee you, it's really corrupt today, but we still haven't seen sin to the extent Noah saw it.

I could give you archeological facts, information I've read about ancient art forms and artifacts that have been dug up, that show we have not seen the depths of sin to the degree Noah witnessed in those days. In less than 2,000 years, sin progressed to a level that, in the next 4,000 years (the time from the flood to the present day) it has never been equaled.

There is a reason sin has been held back. After the flood, God finally did something to limit the multiplication of sin in the earth. He gave Moses the Old Testament Law. By stating emphatically what was right and what was wrong, by giving mankind His perfect standard, God was saying, "Here is proof that your sin is unacceptable."

But giving the Law wasn't God's desire. If God had always wanted to limit sin through the Law — if this was His plan and nature — why didn't He communicate it to Adam and Eve in the

Garden right after they sinned? He was talking to them face to face. He could have given the Law to them then. Why did He wait 2,500 years before communicating the Law through Moses?

The primary reason is because it is the goodness of God that leads us to repentance. God never wanted us to seek salvation out of fear of His wrath, but because of His goodness and mercy. But there is another reason God did not give Adam and Eve the Law.

God did not want Adam and Eve to know the terribleness and depths of their sin. Can you imagine what it would have been like for Adam and Eve if they would have understood what their sin was really going to do to the human race? Can you imagine what it would have been like if they had been given a glimpse of the billions of people who are going to be in hell throughout all eternity because of what they had done? Can you imagine if they had had a graphic picture of all of the suffering, the tragedy, the wars, and atrocities that their sin was going to cause? What would that have done to them? They would not have been able to tolerate that realization. I don't think they would have been able to live with it.

God did not want Adam and Eve to know the depths of their sin even though they were guilty. He did not want to impute sin to them, so He operated in love and mercy towards them. He chose not to reveal to them all of His Laws about how sinful they really were and exactly what they had done to the human race. Instead of pouring out all of His wrath upon them, He operated in love and mercy towards them and their descendants.

Adam and Eve's descendants would have started avoiding God even more if He had made them understand how vile they were. If they had understood God's view of sin, hopelessness would have set in on the human race to such a degree that they wouldn't have been able to believe God offered them mercy or forgiveness. They would not have been able to expect help from Him and would have turned themselves over to Satan.

By showing Adam and Eve and their descendants mercy, love, and forgiveness, God was drawing them to Himself, that they might accept His promise of redemption through the coming Messiah and be saved.

Even when Cain killed a man, God extended love and forgiveness to him instead of wrath. But people began to misunderstand God's mercy and Cain's great-great-great grandson began to justify his sin because God didn't punish Cain. He began to think, "Well, God must not *really* be against it because Cain got by with it." And so man began to see God's lack of punishment as approval, lowering their standard of holiness.

People began to go further and further into sin, yielding themselves more and more to Satan, to the point where Satan was literally destroying the human race. To preserve those who were righteous, and prevent the total destruction of man, God decided to wipe out the human race except for Noah and his family.

In the book of Genesis, chapter 6, God sent the flood as a momentary expression of His wrath on the earth. But even the flood was really a manifestation of His love, because sin had become so bad, God only had eight people left on earth who were responsive to Him. If He hadn't intervened and done something, there would have been nobody loyal to Him left on the earth, and we would have never had the plan of redemption. Because of His love, God wanted a plan of redemption for those who had already lived and those who would live on the earth in the future.

Jesus was God's agent for redemption, and He had to be born of a human being who was not from a corrupted line of people. Jesus had to be born of people who had given place to God and allowed the Spirit of God to work through them. If God hadn't intervened with the flood, there would have been no virgin to give birth to Jesus. Sin had become that bad on the face of the earth. Although the flood was a judgment of God, it was also a manifestation of the mercy and the love of God for the future of mankind.

God showed great restraint dealing with sin from the days of Adam until the days of Noah. He operated in mercy, love, and forgiveness, not imputing people's sins to them. Why? Was it because He approved of sin? No, it was because He didn't want people to know how vile and filthy they were, because the knowledge of sin drives people away from Him.

But in the end, sin multiplied so grievously before the flood, that after the flood God handed down the Law to Moses. Again, this was not God's first choice, but it was the only choice mankind gave Him.

Chapter 3

God's Purpose for the Law

Any person who really understands the goodness of God runs straight to Him when they mess up. Yet many of us, when we get into problems, and especially if we aren't living a godly life, run *from* God.

What's the first thing that happens when we sin and our conscience convicts us that we've done wrong? The first thing that happens to most believers when they sin is that they start feeling guilty and condemned and they begin avoiding God. They know they have broken God's Law.

Usually when a believer knows they have broken the Law, they don't want to be confronted by God. They are afraid He is going to reject them or bring some terrible punishment on them if they go near Him. So they forget their Bible study and skip their prayer time. They avoid church and the people of God because they are afraid they will be exposed.

Do you relate to what I'm sharing? Maybe you know somebody who got into sin and eventually stopped going to church, or maybe I am describing you. When you sin, you may not even think it through enough to verbalize what's actually happening, but in your heart you're fearful of coming before God. You're afraid of having your sin exposed and that God will reject you as a person, that He will find no value in your life.

Then there's the punishment part. Most of us who are born again don't believe God is going to send us to hell for a few sins, but we believe He will not continue to fellowship with us, protect us, or provide for us. We think there has to be some groveling in the dirt and major humiliation to get God to go easy on us. This attitude drives us from God. Where does this attitude come from?

The Law Brings Condemnation and Gives Strength to Sin

We have discussed how the Old Testament is not an exact representation of God, but it goes much deeper than that. The old covenant was an inferior covenant to the new covenant. The whole book of Hebrews addresses this concept in detail, but here are a few scriptures to illustrate my point.

But now hath he obtained a more excellent ministry, by how much also he is the mediator of a better covenant, which was established upon better promises.

If that first covenant had been faultless, then should no place have been sought for the second.

Hebrews 8:6,7

In that he saith, A new covenant, he hath made the first old. Now that which decayeth and waxeth old is ready to vanish away.

Hebrews 8:13

Jesus made a surety of a better testament.

Hebrews 7:22

The old covenant couldn't make anything perfect, so God had to bring in something better. This was the new covenant, which was sealed by the shed blood of Jesus Christ. The new covenant brought greater glory to God than the old covenant.

But if the ministration of death, written and engraven in stones, was glorious, so that the children of Israel could not stedfastly behold the face

of Moses for the glory of his countenance; which glory was to be done away:

How shall not the ministration of the spirit be rather glorious?

For if the ministration of condemnation be glory, much more doth the ministration of righteousness exceed in glory.

For even that which was made glorious had no glory in this respect, by reason of the glory that excelleth.

For if that which is done away was glorious, much more that which remaineth is glorious.

2 Corinthians 3:7-11

This passage of Scripture also says the Old Testament administers death and condemnation!

O death, where is thy sting? O grave, where is thy victory?

The sting of death is sin; and the strength of sin is the law.

1 Corinthians 15:55,56

And this passage of Scripture says that the Old Testament Law gave strength to sin!

The truth we are seeing here is, if it hadn't been for the Old Testament Law, brought into being through Moses, sin would not have had strength to destroy us. I know this may be challenging your theology. In fact, this may just make everything tilt on the inside of you. But we need to come to grips with some truths to harmonize the Old Testament Law with New Testament grace, love, and forgiveness.

What shall we say then? Is the law sin? God forbid. Nay, I had not known sin, but by the law: for I had not known lust, except the law had said, Thou shalt not covet.

> **But sin, taking occasion by the commandment, wrought in me all manner of concupiscence. For without the law sin was dead.**
>
> **For I was alive without the law once: but when the commandment came, sin revived, and I died.**
>
> **And the commandment, which was ordained to life, I found to be unto death.**
>
> **Romans 7:7-10**

Did you know there was a period of time in your life when sin was "dead"? Then you gained the knowledge of right and wrong and the Law came into your understanding. Sin was present before, but it wasn't dominating or controlling you. Sin was "dead."

Once you were confronted with the Law and saw God's perfect, holy standard, you realized how sinful you were. Concupiscence is uncontrolled lust or desire. Did you know that the Old Testament Law actually drew uncontrolled lust or desire out of you? You heard the commandment, **Thou shalt not covet,** and you saw yourself as a covetous maniac!

The Law points to your sin, brings it to life, and condemns you for it.

> **Now we know that what things soever the law saith, it saith to them who are under the law: that every mouth may be stopped, and all the world may become guilty before God.**
>
> **Romans 3:19**

Have you ever felt guilty? Do you know where that came from? You got that through the Law, through the Old Testament administration. The Law makes you feel guilty. It condemns you according to 2 Corinthians 3:9 and Romans 3:19.

Condemnation is not to be confused with the conviction of the Holy Spirit, however. Thank God for the convicting power of the Holy Spirit! He's on the inside of you and will let you know immediately if what you are thinking of doing or have done is sin or not God's will for your life. Conviction draws you to God and leads you in His ways. But condemnation drives you away from intimacy with God and makes you feel helpless to do anything but sin.

Most believers would agree that Satan is the author of condemnation, but one of the biggest things he uses to minister condemnation to us is the Old Testament Law. We frequently rebuke the condemnation of the devil, but sometimes condemnation comes from thoughts established in us through religion. We need to cleanse ourselves from thoughts which have Old Testament scriptures attached to them.

A recurring nightmare I had as a teenager was that I smoked one cigarette and went to hell for it! This is a pure example of how the law condemns us, kills us, and sends us to hell.

Therefore by the deeds of the law there shall no flesh be justified in his sight: for by the law is the knowledge of sin.

Romans 3:20

The Bible says the purpose of the Law is to give you the knowledge of sin — not knowledge of Jesus, God, forgiveness, or any doctrine that is so well expressed through the Lord Jesus Christ. The Law pointed your attention to yourself, your sin, and your unworthiness.

I was taught to do this in my early years of religious training. As children, we were taught to write a sin list. They would give you a piece of paper and you had to list every sin you ever committed. I had to ask for another piece of paper! I probably lived a better life than most people, but I was obsessed with my sin instead of being focused on Jesus.

People thought that if you saw how rotten you were, you would get sick of yourself and turn to God. But that's never the way it worked. By making my sin list, I got so sick of myself that all I could think about was myself. I didn't have time for God because I was so occupied with how much I had failed.

This is where most religious people are today. It's not that they think more highly of themselves than they ought to. Most of us Christians think more lowly of ourselves than we ought to. We're totally self-centered, self-dominated, going around thinking we cannot possibly live right for God.

My early religious instructors told me that the worse I thought of myself, the more I would be broken and open for God to use me. But that is not a New Testament emphasis. The Bible says in Philemon 6,

The communication of thy faith may become effectual by the acknowledging of every good thing which is in you in Christ Jesus.

It is acknowledging what Jesus has done on the inside of you, experiencing the love of God, and a heart of gratitude for what God has done for you that makes you effective. That's the New Testament way of doing it!

But the Old Testament Law made us *self*-conscious. It made us focus our attention on ourselves and our sin. We were so full of how guilty we were. We were condemned. We were under an administration of death, and it totally wiped us out spiritually and emotionally.

The Law and Faith

You might be thinking, "Who cares about the old covenant? I don't offer blood sacrifices. I don't kill goats and sheep. I'm not under the old covenant." But I promise you, your theology, thinking, and attitudes are probably influenced by the old covenant to some degree or another. You may not be offering sheep and goats, but you may be offering works of self-sacrifice and self-punishment to atone for your sin and guilt.

The religious attitude of the Law will keep you from what you should do, from walking in intimacy with God. When you sin, the Law causes you to focus on your sin. And focusing on sin will keep you from entering into the Holy of Holies and calling on God "Abba (Daddy) Father" — which is the only way you can get free of sin!

The Law keeps us from that kind of intimacy because we only see the wrath, the judgment, and the punishment of God upon our sin. When the Law reveals our sin, our unworthiness, and our guilt, we generally run from God instead of to God.

Now not everything from Genesis to Malachi is the Law. There is also a tremendous amount of faith in the Old Testament, but you've got to look for it. This is because the Old Testament was basically an administration of Law, and the Bible says,

> **So then they which be of faith are blessed with faithful Abraham.**
>
> **For as many as are of the works of the law are under the curse: for it is written, Cursed is every one that continueth not in all things which are written in the book of the law to do them.**
>
> **But that no man is justified by the law in the sight of God, it is evident: for, The just shall live by faith.**
>
> **And the law is not of faith.**
>
> **Galatians 3:9-12**

I'm glad Paul said that instead of me! I would get in trouble with the religious crowd for saying **the law is not of faith.** Put that together with Romans 14:23, which says, **Whatsoever is not of faith is sin,** and you can see that a New Testament believer trying to please God by living under Old Testament Law is not in faith and is actually in sin.

Did you know that trying to serve God the same way King David or Elisha did is sin for the New Testament believer? **Whatsoever is not of faith is sin,** and the Old Testament Law **is not of faith!**

There are four books of the New Testament that were written for the sole purpose of trying to renew our minds from serving God under the Old Testament Law: The entire books of

Romans, Hebrews, and Galatians, and the majority of the book of Ephesians. In general, all of Paul's epistles are strong on this.

The book of Romans was written to renew people's minds from the Old Testament Law and works — justification by works and by effort. The book of Hebrews emphasizes strongly that we recognize Jesus has superseded everything in the Old Testament. Jesus is now our High Priest, and we aren't operating under blood sacrifices of bulls and goats, but are set free by the shedding of His sinless blood.

The Church has accepted the truth that we no longer sacrifice animals, but the Scriptures also go on to say that we are no longer operating under that same system of the Law, where our conscience should condemn us.

> **There is therefore now no condemnation to them which are in Christ Jesus.**
>
> **Romans 8:1**
>
> **The worshippers once purged should have had no more conscience of sins.**
>
> **Hebrews 10:2**

The Bible says believers should have their conscience purged to have no more consciousness of sin. That means no more awareness of sin. There are probably quite a few people who would like to stone me for saying this. They are saying, "Brother, how dare you! I believe we've got to keep the Ten Commandments; we've got to live under the Old Testament Law."

A lot of people believe you must keep the Law, but most of them couldn't recite the Ten Commandments. Besides that, there are not just ten commandments, there are hundreds of commandments in the Old Testament Law. Most people don't know what they are, and yet they insist they've got to live under them! At best, that's just being inconsistent. A person who really believes that should know what the commandments are. There are many scriptures that bear this out.

Knowing that a man is not justified by the works of the law, but by the faith of Jesus Christ, even we have believed in Jesus Christ, that we might be justified by the faith of Christ, and not by the works of the law: for by the works of the law shall no flesh be justified.

But if, while we seek to be justified by Christ, we ourselves also are found sinners, is therefore Christ the minister of sin? God forbid.

For if I build again the things which I destroyed, I make myself a transgressor.

For I through the law am dead to the law, that I might live unto God.

I am crucified with Christ: nevertheless I live; yet not I, but Christ liveth in me: and the life which I now live in the flesh I live by the faith of the Son of God, who loved me, and gave himself for me.

I do not frustrate the grace of God: for if righteousness come by the law, then Christ is dead in vain.

Galatians 2:16-21

Did you know that the death of Jesus Christ is of no effect if living under the Old Testament Law is the way to please God and be justified to Him? It makes the death of Christ in vain. You would frustrate the grace of God. Many of us have unconsciously frustrated God's grace, His goodness, His love, and His mercy extended towards us because we didn't understand Who God really is and what He is really like.

Stand fast therefore in the liberty wherewith Christ hath made us free, and be not entangled again with the yoke of bondage.

Galatians 5:1

Do you know what He made us free from? Some people will say "sin," but what was the strength of sin? It was the Law. The whole book of Galatians shows us that Jesus Christ made us free from the bondage of the Old Testament Law which condemns us.

The Law Is for Children

We have seen in 2 Corinthians 3:7-9 that the Old Testament Law was an administration of death and condemnation. Do those sound like things God wanted to do? Did God want to administer death to us? Did He want to make us feel condemned? That was never God's intention.

We saw in Romans 3:19,20 that by the Law we received the knowledge of sin that all the world could become guilty, and every mouth should be stopped before God. The Law gave us knowledge of our sin and it made us feel guilty before God. First Corinthians 15:56 says, **The strength of sin is the law.** The Law actually gave strength to sin.

> **But sin, taking occasion by the commandment, wrought in me all manner of concupiscence. For without the law sin was dead.**
>
> **For I was alive without the law once: but when the commandment came, sin revived, and I died.**
>
> **And the commandment, which was ordained to life, I found to be unto death.**
>
> **For sin, taking occasion by the commandment, deceived me, and by it slew me.**
>
> **Romans 7:8-11**

Sin produced negative effects. The Law produced negative effects. The Law made us knowledgeable of our sin and it made us hopeless about how we could ever approach God. God didn't want to give the total knowledge of sin, but because He didn't reveal His wrath on sin, men justified their sin. They did not understand how deadly sin was, and therefore they were embracing it. They were just living a totally unrestrained life, and because of that Satan was dominating the human race.

Until Jesus came to earth, God had to put some temporary restraint upon sin to keep it from multiplying, dominating, and destroying the human race. He added the Old Testament Law because of the abundance of transgressions, but only as a temporary measure until Jesus could come. God didn't really want us to know how rotten we were, but He had to use the Law to restrain sin, because people had become deceived into thinking sin was all right.

Another bad effect of not having the Law in place was that God was not fully judging sin. Lightning wasn't striking people every time they committed sin. Because of what seemed to be a lack of seriousness toward sin, people were thinking, "Well, I know I should be better, so I'm going to make a New Year's resolution. I'm not going to beat my wife anymore. I'm not going to drink anymore." They would improve their life and start trusting in their own goodness, which would cause them to say, "Well, I'm pretty good. I'm really very good now. I think I'm going to make it to heaven." They didn't consider the seriousness of the sin they still had in their lives.

Today we hear the same thing. People are saying, "How could a loving God send people to hell? God's going to accept people whether they're Moslem, Hindu, Buddhist, or whatever; it doesn't matter. Just as long as they're doing the best they can, God's going to accept them." That's not the truth. It's a deception.

Without the Law, mankind began to start thinking, "Well, just do the best you can and God's going to accept you." They didn't understand how deadly sin was because God hadn't punished it. So God began to reveal His true wrath on sin by giving the Law.

God's intention in giving us the Law is very similar to child training. You can't take a two-year-old child and get him to obey you by telling him, "Look, Johnny, the reason you are not supposed to take a toy from your sister is because God says we should share. God says we should give and do unto others as you would have them do unto you. So every time you take a toy from your sister, you are really just stealing it from her. You're obeying the devil. And every time you obey the devil, you are giving him access to your life. You're learning the ways of the devil, and if you continue in his ways, when you're 20 years old, that's going to get you fired from your job and mess up your marriage. You're going to have all of these problems and you'll never amount to anything."

If you start explaining something like that to a two-year-old, he's just going to stare at you. He doesn't understand all those complex thoughts. He doesn't understand God. He doesn't understand the devil. He doesn't understand resisting the devil. He doesn't understand demonic spirits. He doesn't understand any of it. So what do you do?

Some people just say, "Well, I'm going to leave them alone until they're old enough to reason with." Well, if you wait that long you're in trouble! God gave us a temporary measure for dealing with wrong behavior in young children. The Bible calls it the rod, but most people call it a spanking or getting swats.

You can successfully get a two-year-old to obey by saying, "You may not know anything about God or the devil, but you do that again and you're going to get a spanking." The child may not know who the devil is, but the next time the devil says, "Steal that toy or hit that child," they'll say, "No!" They'll resist the devil. You can get them to resist sin and you can get them to conform to a holy standard out of fear of punishment. This is without them even knowing what sin is or who the devil is. You can get them to fear that rod and I guarantee you, it will get them to comply!

On a temporary basis the rod is good and useful. But in the long run, if that's the only motivation the person has to live a holy life, it is harmful. Fear of getting a spanking is not the proper motivation for adult living. It's a temporary measure we use until a child can reason.

When I was a kid, my mother used to tell me not to cross the street without looking both ways. If I didn't look both ways before I crossed the street, whether or not any cars were coming, I got a spanking. At that age, I could understand that I would get a spanking if I ran out in front of a car, but I didn't fear getting hit by a car, because I couldn't relate to that kind of consequence. What I feared was getting a spanking because I could relate to that! And this fear made me look both ways when I crossed the street.

Today I'm a grown adult. Can you imagine what it would be like if I started across the street and I realized, "Oops, I haven't looked both ways." When I got to the other side and didn't get run over, I just started trembling and said, "Oh, please don't tell my mother. Don't anybody tell my mother what I did. If she finds out she's going to spank me." You would think I was strange! You would look at me and say, "Something's wrong with you. The real reason for looking both ways before you cross the street is not because your mother is going to spank you, but because you're going to get run over by a truck sooner or later if you don't do it."

As an adult, I'm out from under my mother's dominion. My mother's not going to spank me if I don't look both ways. But it's still wisdom to look both ways because I want to preserve my life. However, until I had enough sense to reason, that physical rod was used as a restraint on me to keep me from doing the wrong things.

That's why God gave the Law. It was only a temporary measure which pointed to the permanent answer. Old Testament people weren't born again. They couldn't receive revelation knowledge as we do. First Corinthians 2:14 says,

> **But the natural man receiveth not the things of the Spirit of God: for they are foolishness unto him: neither can he know them, because they are spiritually discerned.**

Old Testament people couldn't understand the things I'm talking about, so God gave them a physical restraint, something they could understand. They were thinking, "Well, sin isn't really very bad." So God said, "You don't think so? You do this — you pick up sticks on a Sabbath day — and I'll have you stoned to death." Suddenly, they began to realize God didn't like the way they had been living on the Sabbath day.

God said, "If you don't tithe, you're cursed with a curse." Then people said, "I think God wants me to tithe." God said, "You kill, and you shall be killed. An eye for an eye, a tooth for a tooth, hand for hand and foot for foot." They got a new understanding of how serious sin was!

When God began to reveal His wrath upon sin, suddenly people began to realize what they had thought was right and wrong was totally off base. Their conscience had been defiled and deadened, so God had to help them realize what right and wrong really were. The Law revived their conscience.

Correct Use of the Law

But before faith came, we were kept under the law, shut up unto the faith which should afterwards be revealed.

Galatians 3:23

People had been trusting themselves for salvation thinking, "Well, I'm really pretty good. I haven't done anything terribly wrong in a long time and surely I'm all right now." After the Law was given, they began to realize, "Even if I never sin again, I can't do anything to atone for my past sins." They began to realize the hopelessness of their situation.

But we know that the law is good, if a man use it lawfully;

Knowing this, that the law is not made for a righteous man, but for the lawless and disobedient, for the ungodly and for sinners, for unholy and profane, for murderers of fathers and murderers of mothers, for manslayers,

For whoremongers, for them that defile themselves with mankind, for mensteelers, for liars, for perjured persons, and if there be any other thing that is contrary to sound doctrine.

1 Timothy 1:8-10

There is a right purpose and use of the Law. The correct purpose of the Law is to give revelation to a person who does not see his need for God. A person who does not understand he has transgressed against God has deceived themselves and the Law can be used to show that they are not going to heaven without salvation through Jesus.

I was ministering in Houston, Texas, when a man stood up in one of my services and started yelling at me. I tried to talk to him, but he wasn't even coherent. Finally I just rebuked him and told him to sit down, and he did. After the service was over, he came up to the front and sat down on the front row. He was totally spaced out on drugs and could barely talk to me. I told him, "God loves you, and God wants to change your life. He can set you free and take you out of the bondage you're under."

The man said, "I don't have any problem. I'm not under any bondage. Everything's cool with me. Everything's fine." I could tell by looking at the guy that it wasn't, so I said, "Look, God Himself can come live on the inside of you and set you free."

He replied, "I am God. God's in the ceiling. God's in the cement." He regarded God as a force and a concept, not as a real person. He said, "I don't have any sin. Sin is just relative."

This man had actually hardened and deceived himself to the point where he didn't even understand God's perfect standard. I had started out ministering love, trying to use the goodness of God to lead him to repentance. But the man was so deceived that his conscience was disconnected. He couldn't recognize a true standard of right and wrong.

When I saw that, I started using the Law on him. I took the Word of God and I began to reveal his sin to him. I cut him from one side to the other. "You sorry scum of the earth. You think you're all right, but you're not. You don't have any power. You don't have any joy."

I began to reveal every rotten thing on the inside of him, lust, greed, covetousness, and all the other sins God hates. I used the Word of God to whittle him down and show him that he needed a Savior, that he was headed straight for hell unless God intervened in his life. And guess what? The Law cut through all his deception. The moment the Law comes, the conscience will snap back to a proper, godly standard.

I don't care how deceived a person has become or how much they think, "Drugs are all right. Free sex is all right. Sin is just relative." You minister the Law to them in the right way, and I guarantee you they will see their sinfulness. The Lord will destroy all deception and cause their conscience to work properly.

Incorrect Use of the Law

The purpose of the Law was to show us our need for God. But once we correctly recognize our need for God, the Law is totally incapable of producing the relationship with Him we realize we need. This is where many people have missed it.

After becoming convicted of their sins, they start trying to get a right relationship with God by trying to keep the Law! The Old Testament Law was full of "Thou shalt nots." People interpreted them to say, "God is telling me what I've got to do to earn a relationship with Him. Now, if I'll just keep the Sabbath, if I'll honor my father and mother, if I won't murder, if I won't steal, if I won't bear false witness, and all of these things, then I'll be all right with God."

No, that wasn't what God was teaching. God didn't give the Law so you could keep it and earn your way to heaven — because nobody can keep the whole Law. Romans 3:23 says, **For all have sinned, and come short of the glory of God.** No one has been capable of keeping the Law except Jesus.

God didn't give the Law so that by keeping it you could earn your way to heaven. Rather, God gave the Law to show you how hopeless you were. It was to show you how sinful you were so you would quit trusting in yourself and look to Him for salvation.

Religion preaches the Law. Religion says that unless you come to church and follow an exclusive list of rules, God's not going to answer your prayers and you'll never get to heaven. But if that were true, none of us could have been born again, because we sure weren't living right before we were born again! The Old Testament Law wasn't given so that by keeping it you could earn relationship with God. It was given to show you knowledge of your sin, condemn you, and destroy any hope of trusting yourself for salvation.

The Law Is Like a Red Flag

If you could imagine an old bull lying in a field, saying, "I've been treating everybody mean. I shouldn't be this way. I shouldn't charge everybody who comes through this field so I'm going to change. I'm not going to be mean anymore. I'm going to be loving towards everybody." So the bull just lays there in the pasture, chewing its cud and thinking he's changed. But just because he thinks he's changed doesn't mean he has. You try to walk by and that bull is just looking at you. He doesn't charge or anything. But pull a red flag out and begin to wave it in front of his face, and suddenly that old bull nature rises up on the inside of him and here he comes charging!

Did the red flag make the bull mean? No, all it did was draw out what was in him. If a person is deceived, it can be beneficial to draw out the negative stuff on the inside of them. If they think they are all right living a sinful life, pull out the Law and wave it in front of them.

I recall an instance when I knew something was wrong between us and some people we were with. Jamie and I had prayed, and finally the last day we were with them, we just agreed together that the problem would come to the surface so we could deal with it. Do you know what happened? A woman exploded at me and started saying I was the devil. She totally flipped out of her mind. Satan tried to kill her that day and it was a terrible scene. But it was good that the negative stuff came out, because we were able to deal with it. It was good because they had been under deception.

These friends of ours didn't understand what had been going on spiritually, but when they saw how vile that woman became towards me, they recognized something was wrong with her and not me. We countered it with ministry and we saw all those people set free. We are tremendous friends today.

The Law was used by God in the Old Testament to show mankind his problem — sin — and to reveal the hopelessness of his situation. This is explained to us in the New Testament, and we see how God will still use the Law today if He must.

It was a terrible burden to live under the Old Testament Law, but it was the best God could offer in those days. Some people may say, "Now, wait a minute. You think God wasn't able to introduce the new covenant back then?" That's exactly what I'm saying. The Bible says that Jesus was born in the fullness of time. (See Galatians 4:4.) Jesus was born just as soon as it was possible for Him to come as the Savior of the human race. Many prophecies had to be fulfilled, certain things had to take place, and God had to deal with mankind and sin in a temporary way by the Law.

Unfortunately, that temporary way has been interpreted by many people as the true representation of the way God is. They think the Law is the way God really wants to deal with mankind, but that is not true! From the moment Adam and Eve sinned, and long after mankind was expelled from the Garden of Eden, God showed His mercy towards mankind and sought for them to come to repentance only by His goodness, always pointing to the Savior Who would come.

Chapter 4

God's *Gift* of Eternal Life

In the fullness of time, Jesus did come. He became a man and lived a perfect, sinless life. He allowed Himself to be beaten, whipped, and crucified, ultimately becoming our sin and dying for us on the cross. But then He was resurrected from the grave, and the earth has not been the same since!

That if thou shalt confess with thy mouth the Lord Jesus, and shalt believe in thine heart that God hath raised him from the dead, thou shalt be saved.

For with the heart man believeth unto righteousness; and with the mouth confession is made unto salvation.

Romans 10:9,10

Jesus inaugurated a new age. Now men, women, and children could not only have peace with God, they could know God. And the transformation of the human heart became the greatest miracle.

You Are A New Creature

Therefore if any man be in Christ, he is a new creature: old things are passed away; behold, all things are become new.

And all things are of God, who hath reconciled us to himself by Jesus Christ.

2 Corinthians 5:17,18

When you were saved, you became a new creature. Your spirit on the inside was changed. That scripture is not talking about your physical body becoming new. If you were overweight before you were saved, you were still overweight after you were saved. Your body and all your physical features didn't change and become different. Your mind didn't change.

Your spirit is the part of you that was changed.

A new heart also will I give you, and a new spirit will I put within you: and I will take away the stony heart out of your flesh, and I will give you an heart of flesh.

Ezekial 36:26

Put on the new man, which after God is created in righteousness and true holiness.

Ephesians 4:24

For he hath made him to be sin for us, who knew no sin; that we might be made the righteousness of God in him.

2 Corinthians 5:21

You are a new spirit who is righteous and holy. There is no sin in your spirit. Jesus became sin for us so that we might be *made* the righteousness of God. We did not get a little bit of the righteousness of God just to get us through this life. We have the *total* righteousness of God in our spirit. Your spirit is as complete and perfect within you right this moment as it will ever be throughout all eternity.

You aren't going to get a new spirit when you go to be with the Lord. You're going to get a new, glorified body, and your soul will be totally changed so it will know all things. In this life, your body has a tendency towards sin and your mind will always need to be renewed. But your spirit within you, right this moment, contains the Holy Spirit, Who lives in your heart.

Herein is our love made perfect, that we may have boldness in the day of judgment: because as he is, so are we in this world.

1 John 4:17

As he is, so are we in this world. It is not "so are we going to be," but so are we *now*. Obviously, this is not speaking of your body or your mind, but your spirit. Your spirit is as pure, holy, righteous, and clean as it will ever be. And this verse is saying your spirit is ounce-for-ounce and molecule-for-molecule (if there are such things in the spiritual realm) identical to the Lord Jesus Christ's spirit! Your spirit is totally His workmanship. It's clean and pure. And if you sin, your spirit never gets contaminated, because it's not your spirit that sins.

Whosoever is born of God doth not commit sin; for his seed remaineth in him: and he cannot sin, because he is born of God.

1 John 3:9

I had always heard this verse was about habitual sin. People told me, "Brother, you can't habitually sin. You may sin sometimes, but you won't habitually sin or you aren't really born again." But that doesn't hold water, because we discovered earlier that what can be called sin is really very broad.

Do you know what sin is? Overeating is sin. Do you know any believers who habitually overeat? You never accidentally ate anything in your life! Anybody who's overweight — habitually overweight — has sinned. I'm not condemning anyone, I'm overweight sometimes too. But it doesn't matter if you're 10 pounds or 40 or 50 pounds overweight. A little bit of sin is still sin.

God told me in His Word that this body of mine is the temple of the Holy Ghost. I'm supposed to take care of it and glorify God in whatever I eat or drink or say. Everything I do is supposed to be to the glory of God. If you're overeating, you aren't glorifying

God in what you're doing. You're indulging self, and self is dominating. Self is still alive instead of being dead!

The point I'm making is that all believers habitually sin in some way or another. So I don't believe 1 John 3:8 is talking about habitual sin. When it said that whosoever is born of God cannot commit sin, it meant just exactly what it said, and that's addressing your spirit man.

You Are a God-Breathed Spirit

The spirit man is the only part of you that is born of God — and it cannot sin. It does not sin. It's the seed of God within you. You've *never* sinned with your spirit man. You're enticed in the realm of the flesh, and your emotions and your mind may get into sin because your will chooses it. But your spirit is not participating in sin.

Your spirit is not being defiled every time you sin. It is not being corrupted. It does not have to be purged. The blood of Jesus does not have to be reapplied to your spirit. That is the concept Hebrews 9:11,12 was addressing. Jesus entered *once* into the holy place, having obtained *eternal* redemption for us. Eternal redemption was for the spirit of man.

Our spirit is the only part of our redemption that is complete now. We have the promise of a glorified body and our soul being changed, but at this moment our spirit is the only part of us that is complete through redemption. But it *is* complete, and it is *eternally* complete. In this life, it is not going to be defiled.

We are sanctified through the offering of the body of Jesus Christ once for all.

And every priest standeth daily ministering and offering oftentimes the same sacrifices, which can never take away sins:

> **But this man, after he had offered one sacri-
> fice for sins for ever, sat down on the right hand
> of God.**
>
> Hebrews 10:10-12

That's powerful. If you'll just think about it, this will set you free. The offering of the Lord Jesus Christ sanctified you *once for all*. The writer is contrasting what Jesus did with the Old Testament priests. He is pointing out that Jesus does not have to be sacrificed ever again.

One of the reasons most of us don't really understand how completely we've been redeemed is because we still have this Old Testament mentality. In the Old Testament, redemption was not revealed completely. Every time you sinned, there had to be a new sacrifice made for that sin. Every year there had to be a day of atonement when your entire sin nature was atoned for. Over and over the sacrifices were made again and again, year after year.

Under the Old Testament Law, the priests ministered the same sacrifices many different times, but what applies to new covenant believers is found in verse 14, **For by one offering he hath perfected for ever them that are sanctified.** And according to verse 10, if you are born again, you were sanctified through that offering!

Sanctification does not mean reaching a place of sinless perfection by trying hard. Some people teach that you can get to a place of perfection where you can't sin anymore in your natural body. But the part of us Jesus sanctified and perfected according to Hebrews 10:10 and 14, is our human spirit. The spirit man is sanctified or set apart from sin. By one offering (Jesus) your spirit was sanctified and perfected forever!

> **But ye are come...**
>
> **To the general assembly and church of the
> firstborn, which are written in heaven, and to God**

the Judge of all, and to the spirits of just men made perfect.

Hebrews 12:22,23

If your spirit is perfected forever, at all times and in all situations throughout eternity, God can look at you and love you even if you've sinned and fallen short in the natural. Why? The Bible says He looks on the heart!

The Lord seeth not as man seeth; for man looketh on the outward appearance, but the Lord looketh on the heart.

1 Samuel 16:7

God is a Spirit: and they that worship him must worship him in spirit and in truth.

John 4:24

When I come before God and say, "Abba, Father," God isn't looking at my sins and the ways I've fallen short. He isn't seeing those things and saying, "How dare you come before Me in your sin?" That's because I didn't come before Him in my sin! I came before Him in my perfect, sinless spirit and in truth.

God looks at my spirit. No matter what my flesh has done, my spirit is pure, holy, complete, spotless, and undefiled. God can look at me and have fellowship with me just exactly the same as He would with the Lord Jesus Christ!

Now, even though my spirit is pure, my soul and body aren't pure yet. That is the only thing that hinders my fellowship with God. And if I'm wallowing in sin, I'm going to defile my conscience and have a hard time walking in spiritual truth.

The Bible says in 1 Corinthians 2:14 that the natural man cannot receive the things of the spirit. If I'm living constantly in sin in the natural realm, I'm not going to feel like my spirit is pure. God still looks at my spirit and it is just as pure as it ever was, but I'm not going to be able to perceive its purity because I'm carnally-minded. I won't be able to perceive and walk in the spirit realm, experiencing who I am in Christ Jesus. I am locked into the physical realm if I live in sin. Soon I start believing, "God, how could You love me the way I am?"

I believe because your spirit is perfect it doesn't have to grow, but growth must take place in your soul. Spiritual truths are already reality and complete in your spirit, but your mind, emotions, and will need to learn and begin to practice them. The Bible calls this partaking of the divine nature, or becoming like God, thinking, speaking, and acting the way He does.

> **Whereby are given unto us exceeding great and precious promises: that by these ye might be partakers of the divine nature, having escaped the corruption that is in the world through lust.**
>
> **2 Peter 1:4**

Simply put, as we renew our minds to God's Word, spend time in His presence, and form an intimate relationship with Him, the purity and perfection in our spirit will begin to transform our soul. And when our soul begins to line up with our spirit, our flesh loses its power to get us to sin. Our flesh becomes subject to our soul, which has become subject to our spirit. Therefore, we overcome sin because we are acting like Jesus.

This is a great picture of being a new creature in Christ, but what happens if you mess up one day? Instead of saying, "I'm not worthy of You because I blew it," you'll say, "God, through Jesus' blood I run back into Your arms and thank You for forgiving me and cleansing me from all unrighteousness."

> **For ye have not received the spirit of bondage again to fear; but ye have received the Spirit of adoption, whereby we cry, Abba, Father.**
>
> **Romans 8:15**
>
> **And because ye are sons, God hath sent forth the Spirit of his Son into your hearts, crying, Abba, Father.**
>
> **Galatians 4:6**

You will have the knowing in your sinless, perfect spirit that you are God's child and He will not turn you away. God loves you and me, His attitude towards us doesn't change because of sin. If it did, *which* sin would change His attitude? Some people say, "Well, brother, it's the big sins." But God doesn't grade on a curve, and He doesn't class certain sins as big sins and others as small sins. To God, sin is sin.

If sin is going to affect God's attitude towards us, then all of us would be in trouble and none of us would be able to enter into that real place of fellowship with Him. None of us would be able to walk and talk and fellowship with God.

Anybody who preaches holiness as a basis of being with or receiving from God is putting sins into categories and saying, "God will overlook certain sins and other sins He won't overlook." I maintain that sin is sin to God.

This brings up the question, "If what you're saying is true and if I've received eternal redemption, are you saying that once I'm born again it's impossible to be lost? Are you saying that there's such a thing as eternal redemption?"

The issue of the security of your salvation is important to your ongoing relationship with God. If you disagree with me on this topic, love me anyway, and please don't reject the other important truths I've shown you from the God's Word.

Security of Your Salvation

I don't teach that you can live in sin, do anything you want to, and retain salvation. One of the problems we have in trying to understand things is that we go to extremes. People ask, "God, are those who teach once saved, always saved correct? Or are the ones who teach saved-lost, saved-lost, saved-lost correct? Who's right?"

I studied for a good five years on this issue. I spent hours and hours studying and praying and asking God, "Which one is right?" I didn't get anywhere, because in the end I could teach and defend either position. Yet I knew they couldn't both be right.

Finally one day the Lord spoke to me and said, "Neither one of them is right." I would never have thought of that. I was always giving God a "multiple choice" test. I would basically say, "God, which one is right? Is it (a) once saved, always saved, or (b) the saved-lost, saved-lost?" I never gave Him the choice of (c) none of the above.

One of our big problems is that we ask God dumb questions. Take Peter, for example. God didn't ask Peter to get out of the boat and walk on the water. Peter said, "Lord, if it's You, bid me come unto You on the water." (See Matthew 14:28,29.)

What was Jesus going to say, "No, Peter, it's not Me, don't come"? How was Jesus going to answer that question? He had to say, "Come," because that was the answer Peter asked for in his question.

Peter didn't say, "God, am I to a place spiritually where I should be out there on that water too?" If he would have said that, Jesus might have answered him differently. But He answered Peter's question according to the way he asked it.

Another example of asking the wrong question involved a good friend of mine named John. He prayed about college for a long time and received a scholarship to Oklahoma Baptist University. He felt totally confident God told him to go to that school. Then, not long after he began attending there, God told him to leave and go to Seagoville, Texas, where I was pastoring a church, and just sit under the ministry and gain some maturity.

John really had trouble with that. He said, "God, this isn't right. I've got a full scholarship. I've made all these plans. I've prayed and I know You told me to come here. Now six weeks after I arrive, You're telling me to leave the scholarship, leave everything, and go down there to *nowhere?*"

Seagoville's not actually the end of the world, but you can see it from there! So my friend wrestled with that for three or four months and finally one day when he was praying he said, "God, if this is really You, why didn't You tell me before I came?"

God said, "John, out of the two choices you gave Me, Berkeley or OBU, OBU was the best of the two. But if you had asked Me where I really wanted you to go, I would have told you." You see, sometimes we don't always give God enough options when we pray, or we ask the wrong questions.

So I was praying, "God, which is right, once saved, always saved or saved-lost, saved-lost?"

He said, "Neither." Then I began to study the Scriptures for myself. I could go into a lot more detail, but I'll give a brief discussion of the answer here.

Finding the Balance

I believe that both teachings have a truth. Once your spirit has been born again, it is eternally redeemed. Your spirit has been sanctified, perfected forever, and that spirit cannot sin. Therefore, a sin does not send you to hell.

Sin does not violate or invalidate your salvation. You do not fall from grace in the sense that you commit what religion calls an unpardonable sin, lose your salvation, and have to "pray back through" and be born again once more.

The Bible doesn't teach being born again, *again*. It teaches being born again once! There is only *one* new birth. You can't be born again multiple times. The Scripture in Hebrews 6:4-6 makes this crystal clear.

> **For it is impossible for those who were once enlightened, and have tasted of the heavenly gift, and were made partakers of the Holy Ghost,**
>
> **And have tasted the good word of God, and the powers of the world to come,**
>
> **If they shall fall away, to renew them again unto repentance; seeing they crucify to themselves the Son of God afresh, and put him to an open shame.**

These verses are saying that if you do reject salvation, it's impossible to renew it again. There is no such thing as being born again, becoming lost, and being born again once more.

The terminology may vary, but some people use the term "pray through" when they talk about their salvation. They are born again, but they believe they've fallen from God's grace and *feel* if they were to die in that condition they would go to hell. So they "pray through" until they *feel* they get their salvation back.

I hope you love me anyway for saying it, but that is bondage! This is a heresy that has condemned a lot of people and it is not of God. Scripture makes it clear you do not get saved, lost, and saved again.

On the other hand, I don't believe that once you're saved, you're always saved without any other possibility. I believe it is possible to be saved and then lost — but not saved, lost, and saved again.

The reason I believe this is that it is not a sin that damns you to hell. If it was, which sin would it be that is going to cause you to lose your salvation? Again, most people would say, "the bad ones." But if sin made you lose your salvation, any sin — even overeating or gossip — would cost you your salvation, and it would be impossible to ever regain it again. Sin does not make you lose your salvation.

The answer that harmonizes both sides is *the free will of man*. You were not forced to get saved. You got saved of your own free will. And *God doesn't force you to stay saved*. Even though you can't *sin* your salvation away, you can *reject* your salvation by an act of your own free will. You can willfully reject salvation and become reprobate. There are many scriptures which verify this.

One of the scriptures is in Hebrews 6, where it says for those who have done certain things, if they fall away it's impossible to renew them again to repentance. I always heard this taught as a hypothetical case, and that renewing them again to repentance couldn't actually happen, because Jesus would have to die for them again.

But that's not what this passage is talking about. It is talking about a person who falls away. They must have had something to fall away from. You can't lose something you didn't have to begin with. The book of Hebrews describes people who have become reprobate or enemies of the faith.

For if we sin wilfully after that we have received the knowledge of the truth, there remaineth no more sacrifice for sins,

But a certain fearful looking for of judgment and fiery indignation, which shall devour the adversaries.

He that despised Moses' law died without mercy under two or three witnesses:

Of how much sorer punishment, suppose ye, shall he be thought worthy, who hath trodden under foot the Son of God, and hath counted the blood of the covenant, wherewith he was sanctified, an unholy thing, and hath done despite unto the Spirit of grace?

Hebrews 10:26-29

This is addressing people who sin willfully after they've received the knowledge of the truth, but also have *trodden underfoot the Son of God*, counting the blood of the covenant an *unholy* thing! This would have to be people who had completely turned against Jesus and salvation. These are not Christians who simply fell into sin.

How Sin Can Lead to Hell

This next point is important, because if you don't give close attention, you will miss everything I've been teaching. If you think you have to maintain a certain level of exterior holiness to maintain your salvation and if you don't, you're going to go to hell, then you'll come right back under the bondage of the Old Testament Law, having to perform to earn the blessings of God, and it will torment you. You'll become your own savior again, trying to receive things from God based on how good you are instead of what Jesus has done for you. You've got to recognize that both salvation and living the Christian life are totally a work of the sacrifice of the Lord Jesus.

You are going to stand before God someday, and if He asks you what you've done to justify getting into heaven, you can only point to your dependence on the blood of Jesus Christ, not to your church attendance, your tithing record, or anything else. But you still need to live a holy life, because you don't want to give Satan any power over you. The most devastating result from habitual sin is *a spiritual hardening of your heart*. If you go out and openly live in sin, your heart will become hardened to the Holy Spirit and God's Word.

> **Take heed, brethren, lest there be in any of you an evil heart of unbelief, in departing from the living God.**
>
> **But exhort one another daily, while it is called To day; lest any of you be hardened through the deceitfulness of sin.**
>
> **For we are made partakers of Christ, if we hold the beginning of our confidence stedfast unto the end.**
>
> **Hebrews 3:12-14**

Sin is deceitful and will harden a person's heart toward God and other people. And the Word of God tells us it is possible for a person to harden their heart through sin to the point they no longer care about Jesus and salvation. Just as God did not make a person get saved, God does not make a person stay saved. It is not possible to "lose" your salvation, but *you could give it up* if you became deceived and hardened enough!

For example, let's discuss the sin of not going to church. The reason you go to church is not because God is keeping attendance and will only bless you if you go to church. You go to church to be around people who are going to build you up. If you are sitting home watching TV, you aren't going to hear the kinds of things I'm teaching, and your heart is going to slowly become hardened to the things of God.

When your heart, through the deceitfulness of sin, becomes hardened, you become dull and insensitive to the leading of God. You start straying further and further away from Him and His protection. Obeying His Word and the leading of the Holy Spirit would no longer be important.

Any particular kind of sin or combination of sins can harden your heart. If a person continues to practice sin, they will be lured deeper and deeper into that sin, and their desire to seek and know God will become less and less. Also, the pleasure that sin offers will get a stronger grip on the person, making it harder to give up.

In an extreme case, a person could get so deceived by sin that they finally reject all conviction of the Holy Spirit and tell Jesus to get out of their life. That is a very serious — but possible — result of a believer who willfully lives in sin.

Ultimately it is possible for believers to harden themselves to such a degree that their conscience is seared. They no longer perceive what they are doing in a proper light. They can even think their sin is all right. They're entrapped in sin, and Satan begins to tempt them to renounce their faith in the Lord Jesus Christ.

Their sin won't send them to hell, but their sin will put them in a place where they are so far removed from fellowship with God that they will be more responsive to Satan than they are to God. When this occurs, it's possible they could say, "I renounce all this salvation stuff. Jesus, get out of my life! Stop bothering me!" Because they reject the salvation through Jesus Christ, they go to hell.

It is not because the *sin* made God send them to hell, but because they threw their salvation away and *rejected it of their own free will*. If they do that, the Bible clearly states it is impossible to renew them again to repentance.

You are eternally redeemed. You are secure as long as you want to be secure, but you can't go to sleep spiritually. You can't afford to flirt with sin and live in sin, because I guarantee you, Satan will put you in a compromising situation.

If you've been living in sin and you've sold yourself out to sin, it's very possible that you won't be able to draw on the spiritual reserves it takes to lay down your life for the Lord. If someone put a gun to your head and said, "Renounce Jesus, or I'll kill you," you would probably reject the Lord to save your own life. Why? Because right now you are rejecting Jesus for your sin. Maybe you want wealth or sex or drugs so much that you just shove Jesus aside again and again. Eventually you could renounce the Lord altogether.

Sometimes people are so shortsighted, they don't see hell coming. There are people who have done just what I've described. A minister I will call Mark was known to be a great faith healer. I have met people who were healed through his ministry in miraculous ways. The son of a friend of mine knew Mark personally and says he believes Mark was born again, had a real calling on his life, and moved in the supernatural gifts of the Spirit. But because of the wealth, fame, and prestige he could get, Mark turned away from God and renounced Him for what he could gain in the flesh. He talked about how he now didn't even believe there was a God! If this is true, Mark would be an example of a person who renounced his faith and became reprobate. Thank God that's a rare occurrence.

Conditions for Missing Heaven

There may be someone saying, "Brother Andrew, I can't accept what you're saying, because if that is true then I have rejected the

Lord. One time after I was born again, I became tired of the whole thing and renounced it and turned my back on the Lord and went back into sin. You're saying it's impossible for me to repent, but I know I repented and I know God accepted me."

For a complete perspective on a situation like this, Hebrews 6:4,5 has some qualifications:

For it is impossible for those who were once enlightened, and have tasted of the heavenly gift, and were made partakers of the Holy Ghost,

And have tasted the good word of God, and the powers of the world to come.

Not every person can reject Jesus and become a reprobate. You must meet certain criteria. This scripture says that first, you have to have been enlightened. I believe that describes a person who has had God reveal Himself to him. **Tasted of the heavenly gift** is talking about the gift of salvation. Being **made partakers of the Holy Ghost** refers to a person who has received the baptism of the Holy Ghost and spoken in tongues. **Have tasted the good word of God** is a person who started growing and maturing in the Word, who had revelation knowledge of the Word of God. Tasting the **powers of the world to come** refers to the supernatural manifestations of the gifts of the Holy Ghost.

This passage is talking about a mature Christian. Only a mature Christian who understands what they are doing can fall away or choose to renounce Jesus Christ and His gift of salvation.

For example, if one of my children had gotten mad at me when they were young and said, "I don't like you anymore. I'm tired of being your kid, and I'm not going to be a Wommack anymore. I renounce you and I'm going to be somebody else. I'm going to run away from home." I wouldn't have allowed them to do that, because they couldn't really understand what they were doing. And the law would have backed me up because they were just a child.

My children couldn't legally renounce me and sever ties with me when they were minors, but if they are thirty years old they can change their names, renounce me, file an injunction so I could never see them, and the law would back them up. There comes a place of maturity where they would be able, of their own free will, to sever our relationship.

When they are grown, my children can't change the fact that they were begotten of me, but they can certainly change any future relationship with me. They have a free will to do it, and they have entered a place of maturity where it's legally possible. They understand what they're doing.

I ran away from home when I was eight years old. Even though I was only three blocks away, I thought my parents were never going to catch me. Although I was already wanting to go back home, I couldn't humble myself and let them know it. So I got myself caught in a barbed-wire fence and I was waiting for them to come get me. I had changed my mind within two or three minutes after I left home. I didn't really mean it. I didn't really know what I was doing.

There are some people who never matured much in the Lord and because of that, they got frustrated, quit living for God, maybe went back into sin, and did all kinds of things. But they had not reached the place where they were knowledgeable enough in the things of God for Him to hold them fully responsible. Therefore, they were able to turn, repent, and come back to the Lord.

And even as they did not like to retain God in their knowledge, God gave them over to a reprobate mind, to do those things which are not convenient.

Romans 1:28

This scripture talks about being reprobate, which is a Bible term for a person who has refused their salvation or has renounced their salvation and now has no desire to get it back. According to Scripture, they didn't want to retain God in their minds, so God gave them over to a reprobate mind. It is as though they no longer have any conviction or conscience.

Jesus said no man can come unto Him except the Father draw him. (See John 6:44.) So God just quits drawing them. God quits dealing with them because they have rejected Him out of their lives.

A person who is truly reprobate has no more conviction or conscience. They know they are going to hell and they don't care. They are no longer convicted. There is no longer any repentance in them. There is no longer any remorse in them. They are miserable and have become so hardened that they no longer retain God in their knowledge at all. So a person who has committed what Hebrews 6 is talking about is not concerned about their reprobate status. They no longer care about God, Jesus, or salvation.

Someone may be thinking, "Brother, have I ever done that? Have I sinned against God to that extent? Have I renounced my salvation? Am I reprobate?" *You can know you are not lost and without hope simply because you care whether you are or not!*

If you are still being convicted by God, if you still have a desire to repent and come back to God, if there is any drawing in your heart towards God, then you are not reprobate and you have not committed that "unpardonable" sin of rejecting Jesus and your salvation.

But I am addressing this because it is possible. There are scriptures that deal with renouncing your salvation, but it is never something that could happen by mistake or accident. And it is never something that happens because of a particular sin. Again, if a sin could cause us to lose our salvation, which sin would it be?

You weren't forced to get saved and you're not forced to stay saved. You have to maintain and hold fast your profession of faith without wavering. And as a mature believer, if you ever renounce your faith in the Lord Jesus Christ, you can throw salvation away. You cannot be *robbed* of your salvation, but you can *willfully give it away.*

Living Free in Jesus

Most of us have not had a correct concept of being righteous, pure, and holy in the sight of God. We have not understood eternal redemption. We have thought that our spirit was less than what it really was. We have seen ourselves as being defiled and we have come before God seeing ourselves that way.

It is true that our flesh gets defiled by sin. This is the reason 1 John 1:9 says, **If we confess our sins, he is faithful and just to forgive us our sins, and to cleanse us from all unrighteousness.** But you do not have to confess your sins and be forgiven after you are born again *to stay saved* or reestablish your relationship with God. If you did, what would happen if you missed one? What makes you think you've been able to confess every sin that you've ever committed? That thinking implies you had better keep accurate records, because if you fail to confess one sin you'll be headed straight for hell.

No, 1 John 1:9 is dealing with the physical realm. There is a cleansing that takes place when you confess your sins. It restores the *quality of your fellowship* with God, but your *relationship* is always intact. The problem with sin in believers' lives is, they are submitting themselves to Satan, giving him a legal right to dominate them.

> **Know ye not, that to whom ye yield yourselves servants to obey, his servants ye are to whom ye obey; whether of sin unto death, or of obedience unto righteousness?**
>
> **Romans 6:16**

What happens if you have yielded your flesh to sin? What happens if you have given Satan direct inroads into your life? How do you cope with it? You confess it and say, "Father, I confess my sin and I ask forgiveness." You are not asking forgiveness to reinstate your salvation or make your spirit born again, again. Your spirit has been cleansed and born again forever. You are simply restoring your intimacy with God and kicking the devil out of your life.

If you are born again, God has forgiven you of all sin — past, present, and future. You may ask, "Brother, how could God forgive you of a sin you haven't committed yet?" Well, you better hope He can do that, because when Jesus died for sins about 2,000 years ago, none of your sins had been committed yet!

Your born-again human spirit is forgiven of all sins and totally perfect. If we sin, we should confess our sins, but not to get saved again! Confessing our sins restores our fellowship with God, but our relationship was never broken.

You will never question your worthiness to walk boldly into the throne room of grace if you understand who you are in Jesus Christ. No matter how big the problem, how terrible the sin, how grave the disease, or how strong the demon, God is there for you.

For I am persuaded, that neither death, nor life, nor angels, nor principalities, nor powers, nor things present, nor things to come,

Nor height, nor depth, nor any other creature, shall be able to separate us from the love of God, which is in Christ Jesus our Lord.

Romans 8:38,39

Chapter 5

God's Grace for the Believer

Let no man therefore judge you in meat, or in drink, or in respect of an holyday, or of the new moon, or of the sabbath days:

Which are a shadow of things to come; but the body is of Christ.

Colossians 2:16,17

The Old Testament was just a shadow of things that were to come. According to this passage of Scripture, it was not the exact image of things the way God wanted them to be. The way He dealt with people under the old covenant was not His preference. Somebody may say, "Well then, why did He do it? Doesn't God do whatever He wants to do?"

I could spend a lot of time on this, but — to put it in a nutshell — not everything that happens is what God wants to have happen. This is because He gave mankind free will. God committed a tremendous amount of authority to us when He gave Adam dominion over the earth (see Genesis 1:26,28), and man really messed up His original plan.

God did not want the transgression in the Garden of Eden. God did not plan for us to go through the Dark Ages. God did not plan for the Church to have the Spanish Inquisition or for the people who believed in God to be martyred. God did not orchestrate these events, and He does not control everything that happens to us. There are forces in operation in this earth because of the place given to Satan and his human followers, and I guarantee you there have been times when God has not had His perfect will manifested.

God's overall will *is* going to manifest eventually. God is going to win this whole battle here on the earth. There's no doubt about that! If He has to raise up a donkey again to speak His Word, He's going to get it done, and Jesus is going to return victoriously. But I'm saying that God uses people — and people can thwart, prolong, and hinder what God wants to happen. I don't believe anyone can totally overthrow God's will from eventually happening, but people can surely hinder it. You can especially hinder His will in your own life. His will doesn't automatically come to pass.

People who believe nothing happens except what God ordains to happen get violently upset when I start preaching this! But I can't understand why they get so upset. If nobody could do anything except what God ordained, then I couldn't be teaching this unless God ordained me to teach it. So the people who believe God causes everything to happen contradict themselves by telling me it is not God's will for me to teach this!

The truth is that not every word said and not every thing done is totally orchestrated by God. Because of that, God was not able to manifest His perfect will under the old covenant as we see through Jesus. The old covenant was only a temporary way of dealing with mankind, and it was instituted only until Jesus came. It is sad to say, but most Christians today make no clear distinction between the old way God dealt with mankind and the new covenant way.

When the Old Testament Law was given, people were deceived about sin. The human race didn't recognize the depth of sin. God didn't really want to, but finally He had to say to us, "Look, you need help!" So He gave the Mosaic Law, which showed how bad people really were.

The Law proved people were totally hopeless of ever achieving salvation on their own. It caused them to look totally to God for salvation, and a type of Jesus' blood sacrifice on the cross was given in all the sacrifices of animals in the temple.

However, as I have said before, the Law itself did not reveal the true nature of God. God didn't really want to kill a person who was trying to pick up sticks on the Sabbath day. It was not His desire to destroy whole cities through Joshua, but the depths of sin in Canaan were so terrible, He was bound to enforce His perfect standard. He enforced it to the letter to show exactly how deadly sin was. Therefore, there was no way you could misunderstand that sin was not acceptable to God in any form.

Enforcing the Law gave mankind a part of the nature of God, that He was holy and no unholy thing could stand in His presence, but Jesus provided the entire and complete picture.

> **For the law was given by Moses, but grace and truth came by Jesus Christ.**
>
> **John 1:17**

In the New Testament, Jesus revealed the *perfect* nature of God. Jesus addressed a woman taken in the act of adultery, which is much worse than picking up sticks on the Sabbath day, by showing her mercy and forgiveness instead of judging and killing her. That's the true character of God. Through Jesus, God was able to manifest Himself the way He really is.

Jesus brought the true ministry of God's grace, but most of us haven't renewed our minds to it. We are still trying to serve God under the system of Law. "God, if I do a certain number of things, then you're going to reward me and I'll get my answer."

Falling From Grace

Whether we recognize it or not, every one of us has had attitudes of law — Old Testament attitudes that have crept into our relationship with God and made Christ of no effect to us in various areas of our lives. The Bible says we have **fallen from grace.**

> **Behold, I Paul say unto you, that if ye be circumcised, Christ shall profit you nothing.**
>
> **For I testify again to every man that is circumcised, that he is a debtor to do the whole law.**
>
> **Christ is become of no effect unto you, whosoever of you are justified by the law; ye are fallen from grace.**
>
> **Galatians 5:2-4**

"Fallen from grace" does not mean you've lost your salvation! It means you are no longer walking in God's grace, but according to the Law. In effect, you are walking under your own effort and your own ability. You aren't utilizing Jesus as your Savior, because your own efforts have become your justification to God.

When believers say, "God, look what I've done," it makes Christ of no effect in their area of need. It frustrates the grace of God. It also keeps God at arm's length in their relationship with Him, because within them is a "knowledge of good and evil." That's a knowledge we have learned from the Law. (Remember Romans 3:20?)

When we have been evil or not as good as we're supposed to be, the Law makes us think God is going to give us the punishment we feel we deserve. Praise God, through Jesus' blood we don't get what we deserve!

People come up to me all the time and say, "This just isn't fair! How come God answered somebody else's prayer and didn't answer mine? I want justice!" They simply don't understand the grace of God. They are demanding justice, but it's because of His mercy they haven't received what they deserve. In a sense, getting nothing is better than getting justice, because if we really got what we deserved, we would all be "hurtin' for certain"!

I used to develop pictures for a photographer, and sometimes when people came in to see their pictures, they would say, "Oh, this picture doesn't do me justice." We would say, "Look, you don't need justice, you need mercy!" Thank God, He has shown His mercy towards us through Jesus Christ.

There are many believers who say, "Well, I don't understand why God hasn't healed me. I don't understand why so-and-so got their new car and I haven't gotten mine. I've been doing this and doing that and I've done all of these good things. This isn't fair." When believers say these things, they are simply revealing they haven't understood God. In fact, by depending on their own works to get what they want, they have frustrated the grace of God.

The grace of God through the sacrifice of Jesus is what brings everything to believers.

Ephesians 1:3 says that God has already **blessed us with all spiritual blessings in heavenly places in Christ.** But it all comes by grace through faith, as stated so clearly in Ephesians 2:8,9,

> **For by grace are ye saved through faith; and that not of yourselves: it is the gift of God:**
> **Not of works, lest any man should boast.**

An answer to prayer doesn't come through our own effort. If we do not understand that, we are frustrating the grace of God and keeping our need from being supplied! The answer is supplied to us only because Jesus has paid for it with His blood.

Justified by Faith, Not Performance

> **Therefore being justified by faith, we have peace with God through our Lord Jesus Christ.**
> **Romans 5:1**

The whole book of Romans is basically teaching salvation by grace through faith — not through your effort, not through adherence to Old Testament Law, and not through your good works.

Paul is saying that when we are justified by faith, then we have peace with God through our Lord Jesus Christ. That is the *only* way you can really have peace with God. Did you also know that is the *only* way you can ever really have boldness to enter into the presence of God? You enter into His presence through firmly understanding the grace of God and putting your faith in it.

If you are approaching God based on the merit of your good performance, you are going to approach God very few times. For most of us, the quality of our relationship with God is based on our performance and that's wrong. If you had based your salvation on your performance, you wouldn't have been saved!

When people realize their sinful condition, whether by the Law or the knowledge of God's goodness, they start looking to Jesus alone for their salvation. But then after they get born again, somehow they slip into the thinking that God's going to move in their lives in proportion to their personal holiness. Nothing could be further from the truth!

I have had people come to me for healing and say, "Brother Andrew, pray for me. I just don't know what is wrong. I've been fasting, praying, going to church, studying the Word, paying my tithes, and doing all I know to do, and I just don't understand why God hasn't healed me." They revealed a lot to me right there, because they showed me they were looking to what *they* had done in order to get God to heal them. They were saying, "God, look what good things I've done. Aren't You going to heal me?"

God doesn't heal you because of what *you've* done. Some of you may be disappointed and think, "Well, now, that's just a shame because I've been doing so good." But if you ever get a true understanding of God's standard, you would realize none of us have ever measured up to God's perfect standard! It's God's grace and mercy which brings us peace, joy, prosperity, healing, and all blessings — based on Jesus' holiness and not our own holiness.

Where did performance-based teaching come from? Believe it or not, it came out of God's Word. It was a misunderstanding of what God was doing in the Old Testament Law. In Deuteronomy 28, verses 1 and 2, all the blessings of God appear to be conditional on the word *if.*

> **And it shall come to pass, if thou shalt hearken diligently unto the voice of the Lord thy God, to observe and to do all his commandments which I command thee this day, that the Lord thy God will set thee on high above all nations of the earth:**
>
> **And all these blessings shall come on thee, and overtake thee, if thou shalt hearken unto the voice of the Lord thy God.**

Verse 1 says that a person has to do all of God's commandments, not just some of them. If you would just stop and think a moment, you would realize that you have never kept all the commandments of God.

> **Therefore to him that knoweth to do good, and doeth it not, to him it is sin.**
>
> **James 4:17**

Sin is more than just doing what you know is wrong. Has God ever told you to love your neighbor as yourself? I guarantee you haven't walked in that perfectly! You know to do more good than what you've actually done.

If you look at sin from God's standpoint, none of us have measured up but Jesus. None of us have become sinless in our flesh, in our actions, and in our performance. We're all still missing the mark. *Nobody fulfills Deuteronomy 28:1 and 2 except Jesus — and those who put their faith in what Jesus did instead of in their own performance.* This is what Romans 5:1 is pointing out to us. We will only have peace with God if we are justified by faith in the finished work of Jesus Christ and not our works.

> **By whom also we have access by faith into this grace wherein we stand, and rejoice in hope of the glory of God.**
>
> **And not only so, but we glory in tribulations also; knowing that tribulation worketh patience;**
>
> **And patience, experience; and experience, hope:**

And hope maketh not ashamed; because the love of God is shed abroad in our hearts by the Holy Ghost which is given unto us.

For when we were yet without strength, in due time Christ died for the ungodly.

For scarcely for a righteous man will one die: yet peradventure for a good man some would even dare to die.

Romans 5:2-7

When verse 2 talks about rejoicing in **the hope of the glory of God,** it is talking about anticipating the second return of Jesus, being glorified with Him. Paul is praising God that one day we're going to be just like Him because we'll see Him as He is:

Beloved, now are we the sons of God, and it doth not yet appear what we shall be: but we know that, when he shall appear, we shall be like him; for we shall see him as he is.

1 John 3:2

In addition, Paul says we glory in tribulations in this present time. Right in the midst of all of our trials and tribulations, we can glory! Paul is making a comparison. "I'm not only rejoicing about the sweet by-and-by and thinking about what it will be like when we all get to heaven, but right in the rough spots today, praise God, I'm a total overcomer because of Jesus."

The point he's making is, "Do you remember salvation — that God died for us? That's the reason I can have confidence that I'm going to overcome in the midst of tribulation, because I know God has already done all these things for me."

Paul is drawing a natural comparison when he asks, "Can you think of anybody who would love you enough to die for you? If you were a righteous man — if your performance was good enough — you might find somebody who would be willing to die for you. But not very many, because that's not the way people are."

Then in verse 8, Paul contrasts the point that he has just made. He says, **But God commendeth his love toward us, in that, while we were yet sinners, Christ died for us.** What he's saying is, God did not give His love to us *based on our performance*. When we were still sinners, even haters of God, and still going our own way, God gave to us His precious gift, the Lord Jesus Christ, in the midst of our sin. He gave Jesus not when we deserved it and not when our performance earned it, but right in the midst of our sin God commended His love toward us.

Walking in More Grace

In Romans 5:9, Paul concludes with his main point,
Much more then, being now justified by his blood, we shall be saved from wrath through him.
In other words, if you can accept the fact that God showed His love toward you when Jesus died for you while you were a sinner, *much more* now that you are justified by His blood, you shall be saved from God's wrath.

Do you follow the point Paul is making? He's saying, if you could accept the love, mercy, and forgiveness of God while you were a sinner, you should be able to accept the love, mercy, and forgiveness of God much more now that you're His child!

As a Christian, you ought to be walking even more freely in the grace of God than you were when you came to Him for salvation. And yet, most of us walk in grace much less now after we're saved. To prove that, just look at how you thought when you were first born again. Say you had come to me as an unbeliever and said, "Andrew, I need to be born again. Would you pray for me?"

Then, as I started to pray for you, God gave me a word of knowledge and I said, "You know what? You're an adulterer. You're living in adultery," and I named other sins in your life. Do you know what you probably would have said? You would have said, "Oh, that's right. I know I need to be saved." It would have made you throw yourself on Jesus and rely totally on Him for forgiveness of sins, because you knew He came to save sinners. So pointing out your sin, wouldn't have stopped you from receiving salvation. You understood that Jesus came to save you *from* your sin, not to save you because you had already overcome sin. We receive salvation totally by grace.

Now, what if you came to me today as a Christian, asked me to pray for your healing and I said, "You're living in adultery." Do you know what most Spirit-filled, tongue-talking, Word people would do? They would say, "I knew it. I knew God wouldn't heal me. I now know why nothing's working right for me. It's because I've done this, that, and the other."

People get real quiet when I say things like that. They are thinking, "Well now, wait a minute, Brother Andrew. Do you think God would heal an adulterer?" My answer is, "Well, I believe if God would save an adulterer, then He would heal one."

Now, I'm not condoning adultery or any type of sinful behavior, but what I'm saying is this: if you could accept God's love shown towards you while you were an unbeliever, you should accept His love much more now as His child. Regardless of what you've done, God loves you even more. Yet most of us believe He loves us much less! Let me give you an example.

If a drunk comes to a service and is sitting in the back, almost falling over, most Spirit-filled Christians would go up to him and say, "Brother, God loves you. God's got something better for you. God will change your life." We will minister love to that drunk and that drunk will respond to it. We would love him in spite of what he's done. That's God's kind of love, so he'll respond to it and get born again.

But woe to that drunk if he comes back drunk after being saved. God loved him when he was a sinner and drunk, but if he's born again and he's still drunk — God forbid! Most Christians would not offer the same kind of unconditional love. Doesn't something seem inconsistent about that?

Grace is not just for the lost. Christians must live by grace too.

Continuing With God the Way You Started

As ye have therefore received Christ Jesus the Lord, so walk ye in him: rooted and built up in him.
Colossians 2:6,7

The principle we applied to receive salvation from the Lord should be the same principle by which we walk with the Lord. If our works were not the basis for receiving salvation from God, why should our works be a factor in receiving healing from God? This Bible verse said we should keep going with God on the same basis as we started!

Some people interpret what I'm saying as encouraging people to sin. No! I'm not saying that. I hate sin. But I claim that the motivation for a Christian to live a holy life is not so that you can earn the blessings of God! Those blessings were paid for and provided by Jesus, not our performance. God does not move in our lives based on our performance.

I live a holy life because I love God, it's pleasing to Him, and because it's my nature to live a holy life. I don't do it to earn anything from God any more than I would live holy to earn my salvation. When you reach the point where you don't care what you get from God, you just want to love, obey, and be close to Him at all times, not only will you overcome sin, but you will see the blessings of God overtake you.

How often did you fast, pray, study the Word, go to church, and pay your tithes before you were born again? Probably not at all. And yet do you think that if you haven't done everything totally right — for example, you have not been reading your Bible or praying — then you know exactly why God hasn't healed you? Do you think it's because you failed somewhere?

I'm sure glad salvation didn't come by perfect performance, or I would have never been born again, and you would not have either. That performance mentality is exactly the reason many people aren't being healed.

Did you know it's easier to get healed than it is to be born again? Yet most people find no problem getting born again because they're putting their faith in what Jesus did for them. They know everything about salvation is based on what Jesus did, and they are not using their own performance as their standard. They aren't approaching God on the basis of what they've done.

When people come to the altar for salvation, they don't believe that what they get from God is in direct proportion to their performance. Yet when it comes to healing, prosperity, deliverance, answers to prayer, and so forth, many Christians believe they will receive from God according to their performance.

I've heard people stand up and say, "Brother, I believe you've got to keep the Ten Commandments of God and live a holy life or God won't move in your life." If someone says that, you can challenge them by asking, "Are you perfect? Do you have any sin? Do you have any problems in your life?"

Then they'll reply, "Oh...well...no, brother. I'm not saying I'm perfect. I know I still miss it." So how can they say that unless they are holy, God is not going to move in their life? They usually respond, "Well, I'm not saying you've got to be perfect." What they're saying is that God grades on a curve. They are saying that nobody can be perfect, but God has a quota He's got to meet because He can't reject everybody. He's got to answer *somebody's* prayer, so He'll take the top 10 percent, whoever they are. I guess they figure if nobody even makes 50 on the test, then He'll pass the top 10 percent. He's got to answer somebody's prayer, right? No, that's not how it works.

The Bible says that sin is sin. James 2:10 says, **For whosoever shall keep the whole law, and yet offend in one point, he is guilty of all.** If you have led a good life and yet you miss it in one part, you don't deserve anything from God! That is what this scripture is communicating.

We need to stop approaching God on the basis of what we have done. We need to come to God for every need the way we came to Him for salvation: through the finished work of Jesus Christ.

How to Be Blessed by God

I was raised in a Christian home and born again at the age of eight, the very first time I was convicted over sin. Now that wasn't the very first time I sinned, but it was the very first time I felt God convict me of sin. I repented that first time and accepted the Lord. At eight years of age, I knew I had transgressed against God and I had done it deliberately. God really spoke to me about it and I repented, confessed Jesus as my Lord, and was genuinely converted. In the third grade I was made fun of for being a Christian. I wasn't doing anything bad, but I changed so much that people could tell a difference in me. There was a genuine conversion that took place in me.

Because I grew up in a Baptist church, my parents knew the Lord. But I wasn't really exposed to the goodness, the grace, and the mercy of God. Instead, I was hammered with, "You've got to live a holy life. You've got to do this, and God won't bless you until you do this." My whole life became one of performing, trying to earn the blessings of God. That's torment, and if you relate to what I'm saying, you know it's torment to try to perform good enough to earn God's favor.

Because of that, I've never said a cuss word in all my life. I've never taken a drink of liquor in all of my life. I've never smoked a cigarette. I've never done most of what people say is wrong. Yet until I received Jesus as my Lord and Savior, I was headed to hell just the same as anybody else. Who wants to be the best sinner who ever went to hell? I might have been better than you, but I needed a Savior just the same as anybody else.

You may be doing pretty well. You may be doing better than you ever have, but you aren't perfect yet. So don't try to approach God on the basis of what you've done. That's the reason Satan has been defeating us — because we haven't been standing strong in Christ on the basis of what He has done for us.

Instead we've been saying, "God, look what *I've* done. Isn't it enough?" And Satan will say, "No, it's not enough. You're a sorry old thing. You haven't done this and you haven't done that." So we're out there trying to earn the blessings of God through our performance. That's not right!

Deuteronomy 28:15-68 talks about all the curses that will come upon us if we don't perform 100 percent of all the commandments — not just 99 percent, but all of them. We know these curses aren't going to come *upon believers*, because Galatians 3:13 says,

> **Christ hath redeemed us from the curse of the law, being made a curse for us: for it is written, Cursed is every one that hangeth on a tree.**

When the Law says that God is going to put the blight, mildew, boils, tumors, and all of these things on disobedient people, remember that Christians are redeemed from that. I know God's not putting those things on me because *I'm redeemed from the curse of the Law.*

Most Christians can accept they are redeemed from the curses, but even Spirit-filled Christians are generally not bold enough to demand from Satan the blessings listed in Deuteronomy 28:1-14. The same Christians who accept that God is not going to put the devil's sickness on them hesitate to claim God's blessings! Why? Because they know in their hearts that they've not fulfilled verses 1 and 2, which say that all the blessings are conditional, based upon obeying all the commandments.

> **And it shall come to pass, if thou shalt hearken diligently unto the voice of the Lord thy God, to observe and to do all his commandments which I command thee this day, that the Lord thy God will set thee on high above all nations of the earth:**

And all these blessings shall come on thee, and overtake thee, if thou shalt hearken unto the voice of the Lord thy God.

Deuteronomy 28:1,2

People have interpreted this scripture to mean, "I'll do these things right here and God's blessings will follow." But God's purpose was not for you to keep all the commandments and earn His blessings, but rather to show you that you didn't have a chance of keeping *all* the commandments of God.

And the commandments of God were more than just the Ten Commandments. Did you know that, as a New Testament saint, you are a priest unto God? (See Revelation 1:6.) In Leviticus, chapter 22, it lists the qualifications for a priest. Did you know that Old Testament priests could not have a mole anywhere on their body? Did you know they couldn't have a flat or bent nose or dimness of eyesight? So if you wear glasses or have any blemishes on your body, you aren't qualified to be a priest.

Why did God say those things? Does He hate people with flat or bent noses or people with moles on their body? No, God doesn't hate them. God loves them. But if you're going to trust in your own perfection in order to approach God, He will show you what perfection is.

God didn't create Adam and Eve with moles on their body. That is something that happened after the Fall. God didn't create Adam and Eve with bent, broken, or flat noses. He didn't create them with bad eyesight. He made them perfect, and if you aren't perfect, then you aren't qualified to be a priest. And if you are trying to combine the two covenants, you wouldn't even qualify for salvation!

God didn't tell you about the moles so that everybody would go to a doctor to have their moles removed, but rather so you would quit trusting in yourself and your own perfection for salvation. He didn't tell us in Deuteronomy 28:1,2 that you have to observe diligently to do all of these things so that you would spend the rest of your life trying to be perfect. As we said before, God gave the commandments to demonstrate our need for a perfect Savior.

Benefits of Obedience

I do believe there are benefits to obeying God's commands. As often as you can be obedient to God, you will shut a door on Satan every time. If you keep 50 percent of God's commandments, you will shut the door to Satan 50 percent of the time. And that is a good thing. The less place you give to Satan, the better off you will be.

It is good to start living in holiness, but remember that you will never be 100 percent perfect. The bottom line is you need to seek God with your whole heart, but never put your trust in what you've done. Just say, "Father, I'm still trusting your grace and mercy for my salvation, for my healing, for my finances, for everything."

At some time, you've probably heard somebody preach, "If you want the blessings of God, you've got to hearken diligently unto the voice of the Lord your God. If you aren't blessed, you just aren't being diligent enough. Start spending another hour speaking in tongues every day. Study the Word more. Do this and this and this."

There's nothing wrong with studying the Word or praying in tongues more, but if you're doing those things to put leverage on God to make Him bless you, I promise you, you're going to come up empty. If your motivation is, "God, look what I've done. Now You've got to perform because I did this," you're going to come up totally dry, because you missed the real purpose of God giving the Law.

The Correct New Testament Perspective

The way a New Testament saint should read Deuteronomy 28:1,2 is to say that the blessings of God are coming to pass in my life since *Jesus* kept all of the commandments of God, and hearkened diligently to them. According to Romans 8:4, Jesus — Who was perfect — gave Himself as a sacrifice so that, **The righteousness of the law might be fulfilled in us.**

Because of Jesus, all of *His* righteousness has been committed to *me* so that the righteousness of the Law is fulfilled in *me*. According to 2 Corinthians 5:21, **He hath made him to be sin for us, who knew no sin; that we might be made the righteousness of God in him.** I should declare that I am now the righteousness of God, therefore all these commandments are fulfilled and the blessings are coming upon me and overtaking me *through what Jesus did!*

That's the way a New Testament believer is supposed to look at it. But when we read something like that, most of us will say, "Oh God, I've got to dig in. I've got to do more. I've got to keep more commandments. I've got to do better." No, that was not the purpose of those commandments. That's the reason God didn't communicate those commandments to mankind for at least 2,000 years. He knew people would misunderstand.

The true New Testament attitude that God wants Christians to have is that God is love and He does not want to impute your sins to you. Even though God wasn't judging your sin because of Jesus, sin was still destroying you, and Satan was not only killing you but also sending you to hell. So God made an atonement for sin. He made Jesus the sacrificial Lamb and put your sin on Him — on His own body on the cross — so that you, being dead to sin, should live unto righteousness. Jesus bore your sin so that, according to Hebrews 10:1,10, and 14, you are now made perfect and sanctified. You should not even have any more consciousness of your past sin.

In your relationship with God, you shouldn't have to come before God and say, "Oh God, I'm so unworthy. Oh God, I know You won't bless me."

Having therefore, brethren, boldness to enter into the holiest by the blood of Jesus,

By a new and living way, which he hath consecrated for us, through the veil, that is to say, his flesh.

Hebrews 10:19,20

You ought to come boldly to God by the new and living way which the Lord has consecrated for us through His flesh. We have boldness to enter right into the holiest of holies because of the Lord Jesus Christ, and to come to God just like Adam and Eve did before they sinned! You don't have to focus your attention on yourself and your failures, but just be so God-conscious that even if you're naked you wouldn't know the difference, because your attention is so totally on God.

Did you know that privilege is yours and that's the way God sees it? That's the real nature of God and the way He looks at you. God sees you through what Jesus did, and that is probably different from how you see yourself. You tend to look on the flesh and see your mistakes and failures, but God looks on your heart.

God is a spirit, and those who worship Him must worship Him in spirit and in truth. (See John 4:24.) When you come before God, He sees your spirit. And in your spirit being, according to Ephesians 4:24, you are righteous and truly holy. You are pure and you are as holy as you'll ever get. Your born-again spirit will never be made better than it is right now!

Your spirit isn't stained with sin. If you sin, your spirit isn't stained by that sin. Your spirit is as holy and pure and righteous as it will be with God in Heaven throughout all eternity. It is perfect, it's in the image of God, and it's exactly as He is. First John 4:17 says,

> **Herein is our love made perfect, that we may have boldness in the day of judgment: because as he is, so are we in this world.**

That's the way God sees you, so that's the way you are. And when you come to God because you've sinned and need forgiveness, or you just want to spend time with Him and worship Him, you're standing before Him in the very righteousness of Jesus Christ!

That's the way God sees you, so that's the way you are. And when you come to God because you've sinned and need forgiveness, or you just want to spend time with Him and worship Him, you're standing before Him in the very righteousness of Jesus Christ!

Chapter 6

The Knowledge of Him

Because we haven't really understood the nature and the character of God, we haven't understood how God deals with us and why He answers prayer. Therefore, we haven't been allowing God to truly manifest Himself in our lives by meeting our needs.

His divine power hath given unto us all things that pertain unto life and godliness, through the knowledge of him that hath called us to glory and virtue.

2 Peter 1:3

God said *all* things that pertain unto life and godliness. Did you know that includes healing, joy, deliverance, prosperity, and anything you can think of that results from our redemption? These "all things" that pertain to life and godliness come through *the knowledge of Him.* If you've got *wrong* knowledge about God, you are not going to receive the "all things" that pertain to life and godliness!

For as he thinketh in his heart, so is he.

Proverbs 23:7

As a man thinks in his heart, so is he. If you've got a wrong impression of God, then you are going to expect the wrong things from God — judgment, punishment, and withholding of what you are asking for in prayer. You'll get what you expect or believe. Jesus affirmed this in many places, including Matthew 9:29,

According to your faith be it unto you.

Many believers have a wrong attitude and concept of God — Who He is and how He operates in their lives. I'm not saying people have it all wrong, but I am saying many people have got things mixed up in their theology. Satan is using that misunderstanding to keep them from receiving the fullness of what God has provided for them through Jesus.

If you can receive this and let God reveal Himself to you in the way Jesus revealed His nature and character, then I promise you will come to truly know the way God is. And then you'll find out faith isn't something hard. In fact, it's really hard to *disbelieve* God once you really *know* God.

For a person who really knows God intimately and has a true revelation of His character, it would hardly be possible for them to believe it when Satan says, "Oh, God won't bless you. Your faith's not going to work for you." The devil could not deceive a person who really knows God and has an intimate relationship with Him.

You know what God is like when you look at Jesus. Once you understand the true nature of God and how much He loves you, the love of God will be shed abroad in your heart. I believe that will help you to have a new relationship with God, one you've never had before.

I also want to say that I don't excuse sin. I'm not saying God doesn't care whether you sin. But Jesus is the payment for that sin, and Jesus has borne all of that sin so that it no longer has to separate us from God.

Getting Your Needs Met

I really believe that one of the biggest problems in the body of Christ is that we learn the *mechanics* of how Christianity works — we learn about faith, we learn about confession of God's Word, we learn about giving and receiving, and so forth. We learn all of these things to *do* and many times we try to put them into practice without really knowing *God*.

The mechanics of Christianity do not produce the "all things" that we need from God for our life. The fruit of the Christian life comes out of really knowing God. Faith comes from knowing Him, and knowing Him is the basis of everything else in Christianity. Remember, 2 Peter 1:3 said that through the *knowledge* of God He has given to us all things that pertain unto life and godliness.

If we really knew God, then all of His fullness would already be ours. I believe in and am not against prosperity, but sometimes you nearly have to overstate things to keep people from misunderstanding you. People tend to put you in just one category — you're either a faith preacher or you're a doubt-and-unbelief preacher. They think you have to drive a luxury car to prove you have faith or that God wants you to walk around with holes in your shoes. Well, I'm not either one of those!

I believe in prosperity, but I also believe that if people really knew God, all the teaching on prosperity that would be necessary could be put into a thimble. You wouldn't have to know all of the ins and outs of prosperity techniques, because if you're really seeking *first* the kingdom of *God* and *His* righteousness, everything else would be added to you! (See Matthew 6:33.)

Many of us have taken our faith teaching and used it to get houses and cars and more things, but I believe God gave us faith to overcome the devil, tear down his kingdom, and get people born again, healed, and delivered. There's nothing wrong with houses and cars, but that's not what faith is for.

You should not have to spend so much time believing for material things. God didn't give us faith so we could have things. God gave us faith in order for us to know Him. Then, because His divine life is flowing through us, cars, houses, boats, and things like that would find us. They would come as byproducts of our faith in Him. They are the extras that come after seeking first the kingdom of God and knowing Him. If we really knew God in an intimate way, I believe God would shower more upon us than we could ever use.

Do parents feel they have to teach their children how to manipulate them — how to confess, ask them just the right way, and do all of the right things — in order to supply their food, clothes, bikes, and all of the things they need? We don't do that! We just love our children and provide for them because of our love. We take delight in giving them surprise gifts.

How much more does our Heavenly Father want to bless us? We need to renew our minds and eliminate teaching that has told us God wants us to be poor, sick, and stupid, but we also must be careful not to focus our attention on the *mechanics* of how things work. I'm not saying that teaching faith and prosperity are false teachings, but they can actually be used to destroy people if they don't have their lives focused on the central figure of *all* of life — the Lord Jesus Christ.

When we are more concerned about the mechanics of how to work Christianity and all of the things we've got to *do* more than we are in *knowing* Jesus, our Christianity doesn't work. On the other hand, if we know Jesus, and we *really* know Him, it is amazing what we can get done and how blessed we become without knowing a lot of formulas.

Never Leave His Presence

When my wife and I first started ministering, we didn't know "come here" from "sic 'em" about faith. We hadn't heard of faith teaching, and yet we saw people healed, we saw finances supplied, and we saw every kind of miracle you could imagine. I can't really tell you how it happened, except that we were just seeking God with all of our hearts. I guarantee you that goes a long way towards releasing the blessings of God into your life! We didn't know a whole bunch about faith techniques, but we knew Him and were continually seeking Him.

It's a shame, but many times when people begin to learn things about God, over the years they start to substitute the knowledge they have about God for an intimate relationship *with* Him.

When people are first born again, it seems like everything works for them. They pray, ask, and they get just about anything they ask for. Miracles are happening, and then after awhile they seem to dry up. They go back to the people who led them to the Lord to inquire why. Sometimes they are told, "Well, the honeymoon's over. Now you've got to start growing up and you've got to start getting things the way everybody else does."

But what really happened was, there was a period of time when their mind was so stayed upon God, they were just walking in His presence. They had a conscious awareness of Him, and they were overwhelmed with His love — and faith works by love! (See Galatians 5:6.)

Through hard knocks, not knowing the Word of God, and Satan coming at them with problems, they got moved away from that first love and began to see things fall apart. And then the religious folks told them that's the way it's supposed to be — that God is doing this to grow them up, teach them, and mature them.

The truth is, you can live in a realm where you are so intimate with God that things will work for you. And I believe that's a way of life God is drawing His people into, why we are talking about knowing God. If we really focus on knowing God, then everything else will work out of that.

We need knowledge of God's Word because His Word reveals His true nature. But when the Word becomes technical details and formulas concerning the mechanics of Christianity, we have lost our focus. We are doing things in our own strength and not His. We are trying to impress Him with works instead of being impressed by His work and Who He is.

If you develop your personal relationship with God to the point you understand how much God loves you, it would not be hard to believe He is going to supply your $20 grocery bill, heal the corn on your toe, and draw your unsaved loved ones into the kingdom.

Those who are struggling to receive from God just need to know Him better. When they really know Him, they will be totally convinced of His love and His commitment to them. Then they will have no fear that He won't meet the needs in their lives.

Chapter 7

God's Goodness in Ministry

Most of us are more conscious of our sin than we are of God's goodness, and unfortunately it is most obvious when we are trying to minister to someone. All Satan has to do is bring up some failure and say, "God's power won't work for you because you haven't been good enough," and we're defeated.

Most Christians will immediately agree with the devil, believing God moves in our lives in proportion to our performance. The moment they agree with that thought, they are doomed for failure, because their performance is never going to be good enough to earn them the covenant blessings from God.

When I stand up in front of people to minister, in their eyes the responsibility is almost always on me to see their needs met! That could overwhelm a minister very easily. Actually, that's an error on the people's part, because it has to be God Who heals their bodies and saves their marriages. My performance could never be good enough to force God to supernaturally meet all the needs of mankind.

I haven't been in the ministry very long, and yet I could name dozens of people right now whom I've preached my heart to and shared the Word of God with, but they're dead today because they didn't take advantage of the truth I presented. There are a lot of people who the Word of God could have set free, but they didn't take it to heart.

I'm not trying to prophesy this, but there are people who will read this book and let what I've said go in one ear and out the other. They won't take it into their heart and renew their mind with the truth of God's Word, and they will die staying in their old way of thinking and believing. I'm not saying that as a bad confession, I'm just pointing out what Mark, chapter 4, says in the parable. When the sower sows the Word, it falls on all kinds of soil and it won't take root in some people.

Jesus said in Matthew 11:15, **He that hath ears to hear, let him hear.** It's true that some people don't allow themselves to really hear the Word of God. The Bible says in 1 Peter 5:8 that Satan is going about as a roaring lion seeking whom he may devour, and there are some people who will read this who will still let Satan devour them. That's not God's will! And if that is why, when I know I'm dealing with people's lives, I'm going to make the effort to get the point across clearly.

For a minister, the responsibility to perform gets heavy sometimes. This has been true in my own life, and I believe the same is true of most of the ministers I have known. At first you start thinking, "Oh God, I've got to have Your anointing." So you start fasting, praying, and doing the right things. But there is a tendency to do them with the attitude of, "God, I'm doing all these things and now I know You'll anoint me." You can begin trusting in what you've done instead of trusting in God.

The irony is, regardless of how much you've done, Satan can just come up to you and prick your conscience in some area where you aren't perfect, and there goes your faith that God will come through for you! If your confidence is in your own goodness, Satan can defeat you regularly.

Satan can send that one person you can't stand across your path and get them to say something that really gets to you! You have a thought of sin towards them, and right after Satan has set you up with that situation, he will say, "You old scum of the earth. What makes you think God would use you in ministry? What makes you think God would use *you* to save or heal anybody?"

When I first got started in ministry, I used to think God was going to use me according to how I performed. Every time I saw a failure in myself of any type, I lost all of my faith to pray for people. I thought, "Oh God, how could You use me?" And for most people, that's probably the way they still think!

Promises, Promises!

Early in my ministry I had a desire to minister effectively, yet I was totally frustrated because I was doing all of these things I just described to get God to use me. I remember going to a Bible study one night when I was pastoring a church in Colorado. I had determined I was going to fast, pray, and study the Word all day long because I felt I needed to. It had been days since I spent much time studying the Word, because I was spending all my time ministering to other people. So I had set aside that day to fast, pray, and study the Word.

People who wanted prayer came by my house from morning till night. I prayed, but not in my personal relationship with God. It was totally geared toward other people all day. I didn't study the Word like I planned. I didn't have a single minute all day long to spend in the Word. I read the Word, but to other people.

A man I had been trying to lead to the Lord came by and wanted to take me out for lunch. I knew that was God's will, so I went out and ate twice as much as I normally did — even though I had planned to fast — and I witnessed to this man. That day I broke every one of the promises I had made to God!

On the way to my Bible study (it was a 45-mile drive) I was feeling terrible. I said, "God, I broke every promise I made to You." Then Satan jumped right in and started reminding me of scriptures. Satan can quote scriptures to us just like he did to Jesus in the wilderness. He began to remind me of scriptures that say things like it's better not to make a vow than to make a vow and not pay it, and all liars will have their part in the lake of fire that burns with brimstone. (See Ecclesiastes 5:5 and Revelation 21:8.)

I was having all of these thoughts and feeling so low that I said, "God, how could You ever use me?" See, I was thinking God was going to use me only to the degree I had performed. I said, "Oh God. Oh God." I was trying to overcome all my failures, so I finally started playing on His mercy by saying, "God, if You won't do it for me, do it for these people I'm going to minister to. What about these people? Don't let them miss out on Your anointing just because I was a dud all day."

After praying awhile, finally I said, "Oh God, just do it because of Who Jesus is."

As soon as I said that, the Lord spoke to me and said, "Who did you think I was going to do it because of?"

I honestly thought God was going to use me because of what I was planning to do that day. Suddenly, it dawned on me that God never used me because of what I had been doing. He used me in spite of my performance! God has never had anybody who was qualified to work for Him yet, other than Jesus. Anybody who gets anything from God gets it by His grace, and knowing that set me free.

Nowadays, if Satan comes to me and says, "Andrew, you're the sorriest thing on the face of the earth. What makes you think God will use you?" Instead of arguing with him and trying to justify myself, I just say, "Guilty! But praise God for Jesus. I tell the people about Who Jesus is, and if they need healing, I'll pray for them in the name of Jesus. They'll get healed through Who Jesus is!"

Do you know that I've seen more manifestation of the power of God since I changed my thinking than I ever saw when I was trying to earn it? Does that mean I go out and live a sloppy, sinful life? No, but I am not using my holiness as the basis of my relationship with God, being used by God, or receiving from God.

The Reason to Live Holy

The reason I live a holy life is because if I don't live holy, Satan is going to have inroads into my life and I cannot afford the "luxury" of Satan putting problems on me. I try to live holy as a defense against the devil and as a testimony to other people. I offer it to God because I know it's pleasing to Him when He sees me acting the way He wants me to, but I never use it as a basis of my relationship with Him. Because of that, Satan can't make me go up and down emotionally in proportion to my performance.

I found the place of peace in the Lord right at the point where I had blown it regarding performance. If someone needs prayer now, I don't look at whether I've lived good or bad that day. I know I can shoot my best shot for people in prayer and get them healed through who Jesus is and not through who Andrew Wommack is. Praise God!

I've seen some of the greatest miracles when I was at my lowest. As a matter of fact, I believe that's what Paul was saying in 2 Corinthians 12:10 when he said, **When I am weak, then am I strong.** Because Paul recognized his weakness and had this truth of grace and holiness in proper perspective, when he failed in his own performance he could trust in God that much more.

When I've been doing everything right I have a tendency to think, "God, You just get me introduced tonight and I promise You I can handle it from there because I've got it together." But when I've blown it in my preparation, I have a tendency to say, "God, it's got to be You!" And that's usually when I get used by Him the greatest, because I've put all of my attention on Him.

God hath chosen the foolish things of the world to confound the wise; and God hath chosen the weak things of the world to confound the things which are mighty;

> **And base things of the world, and things which are despised, hath God chosen, yea, and things which are not, to bring to nought things that are: That no flesh should glory in his presence.**
>
> **1 Corinthians 1:27-29**

God chose the foolish things of the world to confound the wise, the base things of the world to confound the mighty, and the things which are not to bring to nothing things that are. Do you know the primary reason God does that? It's because people who are foolish, base, or despised in the eyes of the world — who don't have natural talent or ability — are the people who trust in God the most. They haven't got anything else to trust!

The reason God doesn't often use the mighty is because they must quit trusting in themselves first. The reason uncivilized people in Africa get healed so easily is because they don't have anyone to rely on but Jesus. They don't have modern medicine and a drugstore on the corner. If they get a headache, Jesus is their only healer. God doesn't use us very much if we trust in our own abilities and power.

God often uses country hicks to preach the Gospel for that very reason. I guarantee you, when you're a hick from Texas like me, then you know it's got to be God on your behalf or you haven't got a chance. And there's freedom in that!

By trying to perform under the Law, we've done exactly the opposite of what God intended. We've thought, "Oh God, now I know what I need to do to see Your blessings in my ministry." No, that's not it. But after we fail miserably, then we know we can't do it and we tend to trust in Jesus instead of trusting ourselves.

The nature of God never was to give you a list of all of the things you have to do. The nature of God never was to stone you for picking up sticks on the Sabbath. Maybe you haven't been studying the Word at all, but God loves you whether you ever open the Bible another day in your life.

Please don't misunderstand! God's anointing is not based on your performance, but if you don't open the Word, you're stupid, because that's where the words of life are. That's where you get revelation of His true nature and get set free.

Go to church, but don't go to church so you can think, "God, I've been going to church. How come You aren't doing anything great in my life?" No, the reason you go to church isn't because God is keeping records and giving you brownie points or stars for every time you come to a meeting. You need to go to church to worship and hear from God, to grow up through relationships with other believers, and to find the place God wants you to minister. Go to church because it will transform your life. God still loves you if you stay home, but you simply won't know the love of God without fellowship and interaction in a church.

If you don't live a holy life God will love you just the same. But if you don't live a holy life, you're going to give Satan inroads into your life and you aren't going to prosper under circumstances like that.

Relationship Is Everything

Sometimes we let knowledge puff us up, which then makes us self-centered and more focused on what God could produce for us than on God Himself. Now, we don't have to choose one or the other. We don't have to go back to the place where all we do is just love God and have a devotion for Him, but don't know what God's will is for our life.

We don't have to live in bondage to sin and the Law all of our life. We don't have to think God doesn't want to prosper us. We don't have to think God has taken our loved ones. We don't have to go back to all that tradition of men, but we also don't have to go back to the place where all we do is just study the doctrinal knowledge about God.

We can know Him *and* walk in an abundant life *and* have faith produce in our life. I really believe God is trying to bring those things into harmony in the body of Christ. He is calling us into a relationship with Him where He is really the center of everything. I heard a song that says, "I would give my last breath to know Him in His death and resurrection." That's a powerful statement — and it's easier to sing it than it is to live it — but that is what God is calling us to.

I remember when I went through the Catacombs in Rome when I was only 18 years old. I read about the persecution and trials of the early Christians. They buried their dead in the walls along the Catacombs because the Romans would have desecrated their burial places. Believers would bring their dead to the Catacombs for burial because it was where they met for church, so they could protect the graves of their loved ones.

There were inscriptions all along the Catacombs, and I remember one of them read, "Here lie my wife and three-month-old daughter who proudly gave their lives for Jesus Christ in the Circus Maximus today." I felt overwhelmed by the commitment that permeated that place. It convicted me.

In America today, people don't like to think about dying for the Lord. We like to think about living for the Lord. We like to think about having the abundance of God and material things. Why are many of us frightened of or unwilling to give our last breath just to know God in His death and resurrection, to realign our priorities so that God is the center of our lives?

If I were to suddenly ask someone to get up right in the middle of one of my meetings and share some of the good things they had received from God, most of the time they would get tongue-tied and not be able to get it out. Why is this? Because the moment they get up, they are self-conscious. They no longer have their attention on what God did, but are wondering, "What are they going to think about me?"

The moment we get concerned with self, I promise you we aren't a good channel for God to use in ministry. I believe those early Christians had lost their sense of self in Jesus. He was their very life and breath, and that's the way we need to be. When we live like this, living for Him and not for ourselves, holiness just comes out. And when we minister to people, God can use us more effectively and powerfully.

Chapter 8

God's New Wine

We've been learning about the nature and the character of God and the reason for understanding His true nature. We have seen how God dealt with mankind from the time of Adam to the present. There had been and still is a lot of confusion on this, and that's why a lot of people don't understand the real nature of God. We know now why most people think God is kind of schizophrenic — He acts one way under the old covenant and another way under the new covenant — and many people try to combine the two, without much success.

We've also seen that the Old Testament complements the New Testament and points towards the new covenant. The Old Testament prepared the way for the New Testament. But if you try to live under the new covenant and the old covenant at the same time, it's like taking new wine and putting it into old wineskins — the old wineskins are going to burst and the wine will run out. It's like trying to sew a new patch on an old piece of clothing. When you wash and dry it, the new patch is going to shrink, but the old clothes don't have any more shrinkage left, so the garment will tear.

That's exactly what Jesus was speaking of when He taught these parables in Luke 5:36-39. The religious leaders were trying to get Him to operate under the Old Testament traditions and doctrines. When Jesus said you can't put new wine into old wineskins, He was talking about the new covenant and the old covenant.

> **By mercy and truth iniquity is purged: and by the fear of the Lord men depart from evil.**
>
> **Proverbs 16:6**

This is powerful if you'll really think about it and analyze it. The first part says that by mercy and truth iniquity is purged. The only way you'll ever be transformed is from the inside out by mercy and truth, because it's the goodness of God that leads men to repentance.

The last part of this verse says that by the fear of the Lord men depart from evil. By wrath, judgment, condemnation, and fear you can get people to depart from evil. So God gave the Old Testament Law, an administration of wrath and condemnation, to keep people out of sin. It dealt severely with people's sins, not because that was God's true attitude or the way God really felt about us, but He instilled fear in us that kept us from going into sin.

The Law restrained the growth of sin in the earth and it made us depart from evil, but it couldn't do anything to change the inner man, to really change our desires and work the transformation on the inside of us God desires. The Law was completely impotent to do that.

The New Testament books of Romans, Galatians, and Hebrews show you that the Old Testament Law was weak and unprofitable, that it is ready to vanish away. Galatians 3:12 says that the Old Testament Law **is not of faith.** Romans 14:23 says, **whatsoever is not of faith is sin.** These are strong statements.

For its purpose, the Old Testament Law was all right, but it was totally incapable of changing us on the inside. Mercy and truth do that. All the Law did was make us depart from evil for a time and reveal our need for a Savior. But when Jesus came into our lives with mercy and truth, sin was purged from our inner man.

New Testament Transformation

A good friend of mine, whom I'll call Jill, has a long testimony which I'll cut very short. She was orphaned when she was six years old. She had two other sisters. Her mother died and her dad couldn't cope with the situation. He became a drunk and put Jill in an orphanage. He told her, "I'll come back and visit you every Saturday." He came back the first Saturday, but after that he never came back again.

Every Saturday she got ready, dressed up, made herself look the best she could, and waited on her dad to come. All of her friends would tell her, "He'll never come. He'll be just like all of the others." But she said, "Not my dad. My dad loves me. He'll be here." She waited year after year, but her dad never did show up again.

Jill began to feel this rejection. She began to be hungry for people to love her. Every Saturday people came to the orphanage to pick out the kids they were going to adopt. Jill would always put on her best dress, fix her hair, and be on her best behavior. Even though her heart was breaking inside, she would put on a smile and be happy, because when people go to choose a child from the orphanage, they don't usually pick the one who needs it the most. They usually don't pick the one who cries and really needs somebody to love them. They usually pick the one who is going to bless them the most.

Most people are motivated to please self in everything they do. That's the way they choose their mate. They don't pick a person they can love and help to be all God wants them to be, but they choose somebody they think is going to make them what they want to be, somebody who is going to give them something. They're like a vacuum, always sucking everything towards them.

People coming to the orphanage were no different. They didn't select the child who needed them the most. Rather, they picked the one they needed the most. And Jill learned, without anybody really teaching her, that she had to perform to be accepted. So she performed. She was always on her best behavior.

Jill was never adopted, but she was able to overcome some of the natural setbacks. She was elected president of her senior class and became homecoming queen. She was voted most popular and most beautiful. She won all of the awards, but inside it was always just a performance to her. She never let anybody see the real her. Her whole life was performing, trying to earn the favor of somebody else.

Finally, she met a man I'll call Ray. He was raised in a Christian home and he had quite a bit going for him. He loved her and they got married. When they got married, she couldn't cook, so she stayed up long hours studying, learning to cook, and trying to come up with meals. Although her cooking was still terrible, Ray would eat the meals and not say a thing about them.

Jill was always performing. She never let her husband see her in curlers or without make-up. She would get up early to make certain she was picture perfect before anyone saw her. She was trying to perform and keep this image of perfection going.

Finally, after a few months of marriage, Jill and Ray got into an argument. They got to talking about it and Jill started crying. She said later that when she cried, she just looked terrible. Her nose got red, her eyes were red, her mascara was running, and she ruined her artificial appearance. She believed she finally ruined her performance.

Right in the middle of the fight she began to say to Ray, "All right, leave me. I know you're going to divorce me. Just leave me and see if I care."

Ray looked at her and said, "Divorce you? Just because we disagree on something? Jill, I love you. It doesn't matter whether we agree on everything or not, I'm not going to divorce you."

The things he said totally broke her down. She couldn't believe somebody loved her even when her performance was not perfect. Despite her insecurity, her husband loved her unconditionally and let her know she didn't have to perform to earn his love. If she was at her very worst, he still loved her exactly the same.

Ray's love — which was the unconditional love of Jesus working in his heart — changed Jill's life. Today she is one of the most secure people I know because she doesn't have to perform anymore and she is secure in the love of God that she saw through her husband. It took a long period of time, but she's got one of the most powerful testimonies I've ever heard.

When Jill was telling her story, I identified with her. I wasn't really performing for other people, but I was performing for God. As I grew up, I performed spiritually all of my young life. I tried to do the very best I could — never saying a cuss word, never taking a drink of liquor, and never smoking a cigarette. I was as good as I could possibly be, and yet I probably felt more condemned and more unloved by God than the majority who were out in the world living in sin, drinking, partying, kicking up their heels, and doing everything else.

I have shared how I used to wake up in a cold sweat, having had a dream that I smoked a cigarette and was burning in hell for it. I also would go into a restaurant and see all these dirty words scribbled on the bathroom walls, and just because I saw those words, I would go out of there feeling totally guilty, condemned, and defiled. It took me days and weeks sometimes to get over the exposure to that kind of stuff. People who weren't brought up in a strict religious environment, under condemnation, have trouble relating to that.

How Much Sin Is Too Much?

Sin is deadly even if you just rationalize it by saying, "Well, everybody lives this way." You may not feel as guilty as I did, but sin is still going to destroy you and send you to hell unless you give your whole life to Jesus and have an intimate relationship with God.

Even though I seemed to be living a holy life by most people's standard, I was under such guilt and condemnation, I had no freedom to love God or enter into an intimate relationship with Him. I was at arm's length from Him, and He seemed very impersonal to me. I knew Jesus was my Savior and I knew I was born again, but I didn't have an intimate relationship with the Father. I couldn't as long as I was under that much guilt and condemnation. It was impossible.

I find this is where most Christians are today, and the reason for it is because of the Old Testament concept of God. People haven't renewed their minds, and they think God is out to get them. They believe the first time they sin God is not going to bless them or have anything to do with them.

If you are born again and Spirit-filled, you probably don't believe He's going to send you to hell, but you probably believe He won't give you what you ask for. You probably feel He's going to let you "stew in your juices," because you feel you deserve it. Most of us believe we're going to get what we deserve from God — except for hell. But that's not the nature of God.

When people are ignorant of this fact, they're continually try-ing to perform and make enough effort to say, "God, look what I've done. Isn't it enough?" It will never be enough. You will never do enough. If you could do enough to earn the blessings of God, Jesus would not have needed to come and die for you!

Now that does not mean you should live in sin and say, "Praise God, I just get my blessings through what Jesus has done. I think I'll just go live in sin since it doesn't matter." No! A lack of holiness will affect your relationship with the devil! Satan will dominate you if you live an unholy life, and that will ultimately affect your ability to fellowship with God.

The thief cometh not, but for to steal, and to kill, and to destroy.

John 10:10

Don't give the devil place in your life. If you're living in sin, you're defiling your conscience and hardening your heart towards God. But God's love is still consistent towards you regardless of what you've done. Now that concept will cause a lot of people to say, "I just can't believe that, brother. I can't believe God loves a person with sin in his life."

Well, let me ask you this. What is sin? Sin is not only the things that you've done that are wrong, but James 4:17 says, **Therefore to him that knoweth to do good, and doeth it not, to him it is sin.** If you use the same definition of sin that the Bible gives, then every last one of us are short of practicing the revelation God has given us. There's not a person who has prayed without ceasing, who has sought first the kingdom of God at all times, who has separated himself to serve God only in every moment, and who has loved other people as themselves.

There's not a person who is walking perfectly in every area of their life. If you aren't walking perfectly, then you're living in sin! And if that's so, and if God can't fellowship with anyone who has sin in his life, then God doesn't have anybody to fellowship with! If God can't use anyone who is a dirty vessel, then God doesn't have anyone to use.

In my spirit I'm totally clean, but in my flesh, I'm still making mistakes. I am not perfect and neither are you. Some people say, "I just don't believe God could love you with sin in your life." Those people have started categorizing sin! They are really saying, "Now these sins are bad enough to get you in wrong standing with God. But these other sins are kind of on the borderline. And then some of these are little white sins that all of us do, but you can get by with those."

That's not God's system at all! James 2:10 says, **For whosoever shall keep the whole law, and yet offend in one point, he is guilty of all.** Folks, that's what the Bible says. That's the way God sees it!

I have never said a cuss word in all my life, but I'm guilty of blasphemy because God's Law is a perfect standard. The Law is like a big plate glass window running across the entire front of the auditorium. I could shoot a BB through it, push a piano through it, or drive a truck through it. The size of the object doesn't matter. If you break the window, it's broken! And to replace it, you've got to replace the whole thing.

God's standard is perfection. You either have to be perfect or else you need a Savior Who was perfect for you. So even though I have broken the Law of God in what may be a small way compared to some other people, I have totally broken the Law of God. God's Law is perfection.

There are hundreds of different commandments, but you have to keep them all to be perfect. If you have made any mistake at all, you're in trouble with God unless you have the Savior. And if you have the Savior, then you're going to get in through His mercy and through what Jesus did for you — not through what you did.

If that's so, then why should people even try to live a holy life? Because Satan will take advantage if you open the door to him even a crack. All Satan needs is 1 percent to get a toehold in your life, and that toehold can cut off your intimacy with God. When you sin and give place to the devil, that's exactly what happens — you give God's place in your life to the devil. So as soon as you realize it, just repent, restore your intimacy with God, and boot the devil out!

Submit yourselves therefore to God. Resist the devil, and he will flee from you.

Draw nigh to God, and he will draw nigh to you. Cleanse your hands, ye sinners; and purify your hearts, ye double minded.

James 4:7,8

This is the new wine: submitting yourself to God, drawing near to Him, and *then in His strength and the confidence of His unconditional love*, your hands are cleansed and your heart is purified of sin.

Did you notice James referred to believers as sinners? Many of us will admit to being double-minded from time to time, but don't you dare call us a sinner! And what is God's answer in His Word? Submit to Him. Draw near to Him. And *then* you can be cleansed and purified — and get rid of the devil.

The Old Testament Law was to give you such a strict standard, that it finally dawned on your lightning-fast mind that you just couldn't do it — so you needed a Savior. This is true before you get saved and after you get saved. Jesus saved you from eternal death and hell the day you were born again, but He saves you from sin, sickness, poverty, and all attacks of Satan every day of your life on earth.

Religion says, "If you'll do these things and keep the Law, then God will bless you." Religion wants you to quit trusting in God and look to yourself. Quit trusting in your own effort and performing to earn the blessings of God! Begin depending on and resting in what Jesus has done instead of what you've done.

When you do this, you are putting the new wine in a *new* wineskin!

Chapter 9

The Power and Joy in God–Consciousness

In the Old Testament, we saw the wrath and judgment of God on people because of their disobedience. He was trying to show them that unless they were perfect they didn't deserve things from Him.

Of course, nobody could be perfect under the old covenant, because they did not have a transformation of their heart. So that is why God had them offer animal sacrifices and give material offerings. But the book of Hebrews outlines very clearly that we have a sacrifice that ended all sacrifices. Jesus made one sacrifice for sins for all time. He has cleansed us so that we no longer need to have any more consciousness of sin.

The Old Testament Law gave us knowledge of sin, which caused mankind's biggest problem after the Fall: *self-centeredness.* People who are consumed with keeping the Law are obsessed with their sin, which means they are always focusing on themselves. Believers like that are always self-conscious. They are conscious of whether they have sinned or not sinned. They are very sensitive to how guilty they are and how far short they've fallen.

Self-centeredness will devastate a believer in their relationship with God.

I believe what hinders most of us from being the witness for Jesus we should be is that we are so conscious of how far away we are from perfection, we feel guilty trying to talk about the Lord with other people. We're self-conscious, constantly thinking, "What are these people going to think of me?"

The way to get bold is to get so God-conscious that you forget about yourself. You can lose self-consciousness in God. You can get to where you don't care about yourself and what other people think. You can be totally God-centered.

How to Be Self-Centered

The easiest way to become self-centered is just by saying, "All right, I'm going to forget myself." The moment you start focusing on yourself and start saying, "Self, get out of my way!" you've put your attention back on yourself!

In my religious background, I was taught to "die to myself." There's a truth in the Bible about dying to yourself, but my idea of how to do it will probably sound stupid. I was seeking God with all I had, and I heard a man say that to die to himself, he envisioned himself in an electric chair where they executed criminals.

Every morning I would get up, sit down, and imagine I was strapping myself in that electric chair. As I strapped myself in, I would name each one of my sorry characteristics until I had listed every rotten thing about me. I kept this up until I saw just how terrible I was. By doing that, I thought I was turning on the electricity and crucifying self. I was trying to die to self by recognizing how sorry "self" was.

But it didn't work. I finally realized that, by trying to die to self that way, I actually spent more time thinking about myself and focusing my attention on my sin than I ever did before. I was more self-centered than ever!

I was so religious, people were patting me on the back and saying how humble I was because I was so beat down. Most people believe that pride is thinking, "I'm better than anybody else.

Nobody's as good as I am." That is one form of pride, but saying, "Oh, I'm the sorriest thing that ever walked on the face of the earth!" is a higher form of pride.

Most Christians think, "Well, brother, that's not pride — that's something else." No, in its simplest terms pride is self-centeredness. And whether you're self-centered by thinking, "I'm better than everybody else," or you're self-centered by thinking, "I'm worse than everybody else," you're still self-centered. And self-centeredness is pride.

You can get more self-centered through thinking you're the scum of the earth than you ever could by thinking you're better than everybody else. This is because it's a lot easier to relate to being worse than everybody else than it is to being better than everybody else.

It's easy to assume that eventually somebody better than you is going to come along, but if you are really down on yourself, you can believe nobody worse will ever come along! Or at least you won't know somebody is worse than you, because you think you know yourself better than you know the other person!

How to Lose Self-Centeredness

Instead of dying to self, I was actually resurrecting and glorifying self by focusing attention on myself. The way you die to self is to get your attention so much on someone else that you forget about yourself — like when you fall in love.

When you fall in love with a person, you get so conscious of them that you totally forget about yourself. You'll say and do things you would never do under normal circumstances. When you are in love, you can get so conscious of the other person that you actually forget about yourself.

I used to pour cement before I became a minister. My boss was a Christian and my best friend was on the crew. We probably led an average of one person a day to the Lord — cement truck drivers, people who sold us refreshments, and others. But most of the workers on the crew were not saved, and we were constantly witnessing to them. They just couldn't get over how much of a "Puritan" I was, and they were always trying to find something wrong with me. They were always trying to give me a hard time.

When my wife Jamie and I were first going together and engaged to be married, they just couldn't believe I was keeping myself honest and pure through the whole relationship. They would give me a hard time every day at work and say, "Uh-huh, you were out playing licky-face last night!" They were always accusing me, poking fun at me, and trying to get me mad at them.

The truth was that Jamie and I were engaged to be married before we ever even held hands. It was amazing how God put us together, and I was so obviously in love with her that the guys on the crew continuously razzed me. So I avoided the subject and tried not to mention or talk about Jamie on the job at all.

One day it was really hot and I was troweling the concrete where a bay window would be installed. As I worked, the water was floating to the top of the cement until I could see my reflection in it. As I was sitting there working, I realized I was saying, "Jamie, I love you," over and over. I was saying it out loud. I was thinking it at first and then I had started actually saying, "Jamie, I love you." Then I looked down into the water and saw not only my own face, but all these other faces around me! They *really* gave me a hard time after that!

I would have never been saying something like that if I had been self-conscious. But I was so into thinking about Jamie that I literally lost consciousness of myself. Do you know that's how it should be with the Lord in your life? The way you die to yourself isn't by thinking, "You sorry thing," and focusing your attention on yourself. The way to die to yourself is to get your mind so on God and about who God is that you literally lose consciousness of yourself.

You can lose your self-consciousness in God. On March 23, 1968, I had an experience with the Lord, and through it God changed my life. I became so consumed with how much God loved me that I honestly just lost conscious contact with the world. It was four-and-a-half months later before I remembered that there was a television or a radio. I didn't even have any knowledge about what I was doing. I became totally oblivious to myself.

I'm an introvert by nature. When I was in high school, someone would say "Good morning!" to me and it would be two blocks later before I could manage to say "Good morning!" back. I just couldn't talk to people or relate to people because I was so introverted. Yet when I saw how much God loved me, I became so consumed with God's love and what He had done for me that I didn't even think about myself.

I changed to the point where I would grab people coming out of the convenience stores if they had a pack of cigarettes or a case of beer and say, "You're going to hell and you need Jesus!" I would do that right in front of everybody present. Now, that's not the best way to witness, and God has given me wisdom since then, but what I am saying is that there was a total transformation in me. I totally forgot about myself by recognizing how much God loved me. God's love transformed my life.

The Old Testament Law never did that. The Law never changed me. The Law only made me conscious of how much of a sinner I was because it was an administration of death and condemnation. The Law kept me from engaging in some sins, but I was still totally self-centered. And being trapped in self-centeredness is bondage.

God set me free by revealing His unconditional love for me. Love did not encourage me to live in sin. In fact, I started living an even holier life than I did before. I lived a holier life, but the difference was that now I was doing it out of love for God instead of doing it to try to earn the blessings of God.

God's Love

If you understand what I'm talking about, then you will understand that getting out from under the Old Testament Law is not going to free you *to* sin — it will free you *from* sin. The sins you have committed won't weigh you down or make you feel defeated and negative anymore. God's love will throw all that sin behind you. God's love will break the dominion of that sin over you so you can start seeking and pursuing His will for your life. Praise the Lord!

But Christ being come an high priest of good things to come, by a greater and more perfect tabernacle, not made with hands, that is to say, not of this building;

Neither by the blood of goats and calves, but by his own blood he entered in once into the holy place, having obtained eternal redemption for us.

For if the blood of bulls and of goats, and the ashes of an heifer sprinkling the unclean, sanctifieth to the purifying of the flesh:

How much more shall the blood of Christ, who through the eternal Spirit offered himself without spot to God, purge your conscience from dead works to serve the living God?

Hebrews 9:11-14

Jesus entered *once* into the holy place. He didn't enter many times, but once, and He obtained eternal redemption for us. That's important. Then verse 13 talks about the Old Testament administration. Those sacrifices could atone for the sins of the Old Testament believers, but they couldn't purify their spirits.

To be God-centered instead of self-centered, you've got to have your conscience purged from dead works, from feelings of guilt, condemnation, and inadequacy. Only the sacrifice of Jesus is fully capable of doing that.

In the flesh, I recognize I'm inadequate, but in the spirit man within, God has equipped me and I've got all Jesus provided. Christians walk in varying degrees of that power, but all believers have the standard equipment. God doesn't have stripped-down models.

All of us came with full provision for everything through Jesus. Because of that, we can and should have our consciences purged from dead works. We should be purged from sin-consciousness and self-consciousness and be totally God-conscious.

> **For the law having a shadow of good things to come, and not the very image of the things, can never with those sacrifices which they offered year by year continually make the comers thereunto perfect.**
>
> **For then would they not have ceased to be offered? because that the worshippers once purged should have had no more conscience of sins.**
>
> **Hebrews 10:1,2**

If the Old Testament sacrifices could have really done what they were picturing, then they would have ceased to be offered. The picture that was given through the Old Testament sacrifices was a cleansing of sin. If those sacrifices had really worked, then they would have ceased to be offered because the worshippers would have been purged and would have had no more consciousness of their sin.

> **But in those sacrifices there is a remembrance again made of sins every year.**
>
> **For it is not possible that the blood of bulls and of goats should take away sins.**
>
> **Wherefore when he cometh into the world, he saith, Sacrifice and offering thou wouldest not, but a body hast thou prepared me:**
>
> **In burnt offerings and sacrifices for sin thou hast had no pleasure.**

> **Then said I, Lo, I come (in the volume of the book it is written of me,) to do thy will, O God.**
>
> **Above when he said, Sacrifice and offering and burnt offerings and offering for sin thou wouldest not, neither hadst pleasure therein; which are offered by the law;**
>
> **Then said he, Lo, I come to do thy will, O God. He taketh away the first, that he may establish the second.**
>
> **Hebrews 10:3-9**

To summarize this passage of Scripture, what the Old Testament sacrifices couldn't do, Jesus did do! If the Old Testament sacrifices could have worked, they would have purged your conscience to such a degree that you would have had no more consciousness or awareness of sin. The Old Testament sacrifices couldn't do it, but the New Testament sacrifice of Jesus did.

Your inheritance through Jesus is that you can be so God-conscious, so loved, so forgiven, and so cleansed of your sin, that you are able to approach God without any awareness of sin.

Some people might say, "Aw, brother, I just can't relate to that. I believe when we come before God we've got to start confessing our sin." Do you know why prayer is drudgery for most people? Because instead of coming to fellowship with God and to worship Him for Who He is, we come in and immediately start telling Him who we are and what we've done wrong — dragging up all of this old trash and reminding ourselves how rotten and unworthy we are. As a result, our prayer time is not that pleasant. After a little bit of that, it's going to be drudgery.

Anybody would rather watch a football game than go into prayer and remember how rotten they are all the time. Maybe you've got something you need to pray about, but you watch a ball game instead. Why? Because between every play the commentators don't say, "You sorry thing. You've sinned against God. You haven't paid your tithes this week. You haven't been living right.

You haven't been treating your wife the way you should or spending time with your kids."

If sports commentators started telling you every rotten thing about you between every play, you would turn the game off. And the commercials minister to you also. They try to tell you whatever makes you feel good so you'll buy their products. They usually make you laugh and feel good, so you would rather escape into TV than hear how rotten you are in prayer.

Sometimes it's necessary to confess your sins, but it never feels good. And I guarantee you, if your relationship with God always revolves around coming before Him and telling Him how sorry you are, then you're not going to enjoy spending time with Him.

God doesn't desire that, but that's the way most of us have been conditioned to think. If that's the attitude you've adopted, the devil doesn't have to condemn you because you're already doing such a good job of condemning yourself!

Most of us have been so religiously taught that we'll come in to pray, lay ourselves down like a rug, walk all over ourselves, spit on ourselves, and talk about how terrible and rotten we are. Then we wonder why we don't enjoy the presence of God any more than we do!

If you haven't already, why not come into His presence, let Him love you, and just start praising Him for Who He is right now? You're His child and He loves you — no matter what has gone on since your last prayer time!

Conclusion

What I've presented is really very simple and every Christian deserves to know it. It is sad to say, but I think not more than one out of a thousand Christians has this accurate concept of the nature of God.

Most of us approached God without recognizing our redemption and what Jesus really did for us. We were in a constant mode of trying to perform. And as soon as Satan pointed out something we did wrong, we started condemning ourselves and saying, "God, I know why it wasn't working." We've been putting faith in what we did instead of putting faith in what Jesus did.

Do you know why it was so easy for you to get born again? Because you were told that it was totally based on what Jesus had done for you — it wasn't your goodness, Bible study, prayer, church attendance, or tithes that qualified you to receive salvation. It was totally based on what Jesus did, on His merits and His goodness alone. So you were able to put your faith in Jesus, regardless of how bad you were, and receive the greatest miracle that could ever happen.

But when it comes to healing, prosperity, or deliverance, we tend to look at what we've done and say, "God, I've been doing the best I can, is it enough?" No, it's not enough and it never will be!

We have been studying the Word, praying in tongues, and doing all kinds of spiritual things we ought to do. But we need to do them to build *ourselves* up and know Him better, not to try to make Him want to bless us or to give Him a better impression of us. We should do these things to stay strong and finish strong in this spiritual race. The reason I confess the Word of God or pray in tongues is not to move God, *but to move myself closer to Him.* Holiness doesn't change God's attitude towards me, but it changes my attitude towards Him.

And they overcame him by the blood of the Lamb, and by the word of their testimony; and they loved not their lives unto the death.

Revelation 12:11

I overcome the devil by the blood of the Lamb, and by the word of my testimony (or profession of faith in that blood). I don't overcome the devil because I have impressed God with my works. I'm not twisting God's arm with my prayers and God is not impressed with my great ability to confess His Word. I've known some people who didn't even know how to confess the Word of God but they saw miracles happen because their hearts were right. Receiving from God will work better if your heart is right *and* you confess the Word of God, but God looks on the heart.

The reason people are able to receive things from God at salvation so easily is because their faith is totally in Jesus. But after we are born again, we tend to start trusting ourselves, and that's bondage. I'm convinced that even though people have committed their lives to the Lord, are born again, and know God loves them, they aren't experiencing that love because they are walking in what they have done instead of walking in God's love towards them.

Does that describe you? Do you see Jesus loving you unconditionally? Or, do you feel Jesus loves you in proportion to what you "deserve"? If you feel you don't deserve much, then you won't open yourself up to let God really love you.

God wants to call us into a secret place of close, intimate communion with Him. He longs for it. God longs for you, but perhaps you haven't allowed yourself to approach God because you don't feel worthy. You may believe if you really got that close, you would be like a hypocrite coming before Him and He would chastise you, scold you, and say, "How dare you think you have the right to enter into My presence, you sorry worm?"

You may not put it in exactly those words, but perhaps that is your concept. Hear this: God is looking on your heart. God is looking on your spirit man within you. And in your spirit man, you are righteous, holy, and pure! You can come and prop your feet up before God and say, "Papa, Father" or "Abba, Father." You can relate to Him in an intimate, personal way.

God loves you, and many of us have been kept out of that intimate relationship because of a sin-consciousness — our conscience has been remembering and is obsessed with our sin. We've been looking at ourselves as sinners when the Bible makes it clear that if we really understood redemption, we should have no more consciousness of sin.

> **Let us therefore come boldly unto the throne of grace, that we may obtain mercy, and find grace to help in time of need.**
>
> **Hebrews 4:16**

You can come boldly before the throne of grace to obtain mercy and help in your time of need, not just when you're perfect and everything's going right, but even in the time when you've blown it and you're in trouble. It's the throne of *grace*, not the throne of *works* or the throne of *perfect performance*. You can do that right now and let God begin to love you.

You may need to humble yourself before God, saying something like, "Father, I'm sorry. I have done everything in my own effort. I've misunderstood You. I thought I had to earn Your blessings. I've been trying to perform. I thought You only gave me things I deserved and I haven't been depending on Jesus. I've been trying to approach You on my own merit."

Confess it to God, fall before Him, and repent, saying, "Father, I'm sorry." Start speaking what God's Word says to yourself. "Father, I thank You that You do love me, that You see me clean, pure, and holy."

Sometimes I look in a mirror, eyeball to eyeball with myself, and I point to myself and say, "Andrew, God loves you. You're holy. You're pure, just as if you never sinned." It's possible that when you first say that, the hair will stand up on the back of your neck because you're thinking, "Oh, God, don't strike me dead for saying this." But after awhile, as you keep saying it by faith, knowing it's God's Word, it will minister to you and you will begin to believe it. You'll begin to believe God really loves you and you'll get to the point where you can't wait to go right into His throne room!

If an angel stood in your way and said, "What makes you think you're worthy to come in here?" You could rebuke him and tell him, "Get out of my way! Through the blood of Jesus I'm righteous, I'm holy, and I'm pure, and I'm God's child. You have no right to stop me."

When you come into the presence of God, thank Him that you are who He says you are. Focus on Him and let Him minister to you. Then you'll begin to be like Him and have no desire to live in sin. You'll start reflecting holiness and end up living closer to Him.

Suddenly, instead of it being drudgery to try to separate yourself from the TV to spend time with God, you'll say, "Who needs the TV?" You'll find those carnal things will just fall by the wayside. You'll find it won't be hard to spend time studying the Word and praying, because you are spending time with Him.

I read a story about an older man who lived in the 1800s. He told his servant to come get him in fifteen minutes when supper was going to be ready. The older man said, "I'm going to be praying in the parlor, so come get me when fifteen minutes is up."

Three and a half hours later, the servant finally forced himself to go in and interrupt this man. The food had been ready for hours, but the man was praying so intensely on his knees, with his hands up worshipping God, that the servant felt it would be a mockery to interrupt him.

Finally, the servant went in and tapped the older man on the shoulder. The man turned around and said, "Oh, is fifteen minutes up? My, time goes so fast when you're in the presence of God."

For most of us, however, praying fifteen minutes can seem like three and a half hours! It is because we haven't really tapped into the love of God. Our wrong thinking about God has kept us from understanding His love, and our religious traditions and incorrect concepts of God have kept us at arm's length from Him.

If you understand what I have presented in this book, it will help you to enter boldly into the Holy of Holies by a new and living way God provided for us through Jesus. It will give you boldness. And as you begin to pray and fellowship with God, you'll find that praising God for an hour or more is not a drudgery, but a pleasure. It's a pleasure because you know what God has done for you. I know God wants to draw you unto Himself right now as you are reading these words.

We have been learning about having a relationship with God, abiding in Him, and coming to really know Him. I may have approached it in a way that seemed strange to you, but I firmly believe when you really know what God is like — His nature, character, and person — you will love Him.

I believe the only reason you or I haven't loved Him more is because God has been misrepresented and we have misunderstood Him. Because of that, we haven't entered into that loving, close relationship He desires to have with us. If we can receive what is presented in this book, I know it will set us free to enjoy a fulfilling and totally satisfying relationship with our Father God.

About the Author

Andrew Wommack was brought up in a Christian home in Arlington, Texas, and made a total commitment of his life to the Lord at a very early age. But it was not until he received the baptism of the Holy Spirit as a teenager that he began to experience the power of God in his life.

Since that time, he has served as pastor of three churches in progressive steps to the ministry God has called him to fulfill: teaching the entire body of Christ the good news of our New Testament relationship with Jesus Christ.

Andrew is fulfilling this calling as he travels throughout the world sharing the simple truths of God's Word with people of various backgrounds. He is heard on radio stations across America and has distributed over 2,500,000 cassette tapes free of charge.

Other books by Andrew Wommack
Living in the Balance of Grace and Faith

To contact Andrew Wommack, write:
Andrew Wommack Ministries
P. O. Box 3333
Colorado Springs, Colorado 80934-3333

In Europe, write:
Andrew Wommack Ministries of Europe
P. O. Box 35
Coventry, CV1 2NE
England

Please include your prayer requests
and comments when you write.

**Copies of this book are available
from your local bookstore.**

ALBURY PUBLISHING
P. O. Box 470406
Tulsa, Oklahoma 74147-0406

In Canada contact:
Word Alive
P. O. Box 670
Niverville, Manitoba
Canada ROA 1EO